introduction to
animal physiology

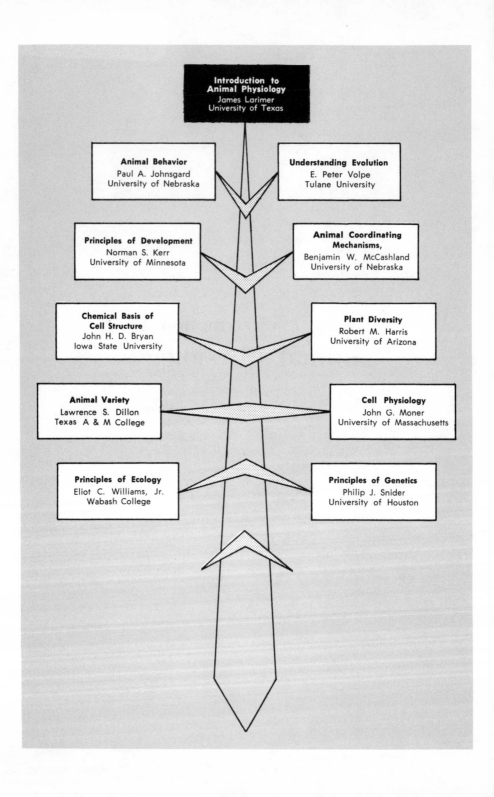

Biology today is in the midst of profound and exciting revelations. This has resulted in a spectacular surge of biological knowledge and the consequent need for new approaches to the teaching of biology. The **Concepts of Biology Series,** designed for the introductory course, transmits the excitement of biology to the college student seeking a liberal education. The underlying theme of each book in the series is to foster an awareness of biology as an imaginative, evolving science. While the individual titles are self-contained, collectively they comprise a modern synthesis of major biological principles.

introduction to
animal physiology

JAMES LARIMER
University of Texas

WM. C. BROWN COMPANY PUBLISHERS
Dubuque, Iowa

Printed in the United States of America

Preface

This book attempts to present some of the basic principles of physiology and to convey an idea of the relationship between physiology and the other disciplines of biology. It has been made intentionally broad in coverage to impress the beginning student with the wide variety of topics that fall under the general heading of animal physiology. Indeed, it is difficult to limit the field of physiology since it grades almost imperceptibly into virtually every other area of biology. In spite of attempts at breadth, several topics of central importance have not been included. Certain aspects of biochemistry, intermediary metabolism and molecular biology have been omitted because of space limitations and because they are adequately covered in other books in the Concepts of Biology Series.

There are cogent arguments for the thesis that every science student should know and appreciate the functioning of living organisms. For one, living things as mechanical systems are often more complex and in many ways more interesting than anything man's technology has yet produced. From our experience we know that living organisms are self-repairing and self-reproducing. In addition, living organisms are also adaptive and this is indeed an accomplishment for any mechanical device. Man-made machines, impressive as they are, fail to achieve the excellence of many of their living equivalents. Consider the eye or the ear as a sensing device, a muscle as an energy converter, or a capillary bed as a miniature but highly efficient pipeline. Think for a moment of the aerodynamic efficiency of birds and insects and the hydrodynamic excellence of fish and porpoises. Even our computers cannot yet measure up to a brain in terms of flexibility and utility. Thus physiology should appeal not only to the incipient biologist, but also to the engineer, the physical scientist, the psychologist as well as others. It is hoped that this book will help to persuade some students to choose the biological sciences as their major interest and will give the remaining students an appreciation for, and an interest in, living organisms.

I wish to thank the authors and publishers who permitted the use of several figures in the text. I would also like to extend my appreciation to Mrs. Pauline West who prepared the original illustrations. It is a special pleasure to express my thanks to my wife for her continuing help throughout the preparation of the manuscript.

J.L.L.

Contents

CHAPTER 1

An introduction
to the study of
animal physiology

WHAT IS PHYSIOLOGY

Physiology has emerged as the discipline of biology that is concerned with the functional basis of anatomy. In a broad sense, the morphological observations of physiology are taken from biology, with the explanations of functions being derived to a large extent from chemistry and physics. At the turn of this century, most physiologists were primarily concerned with explaining the operations of man's morphology because of the direct importance this information had for medicine. Although medical physiology continues to make rapid progress, the field as a whole has expanded during the past seventy years until studies on the physiology of man are considered a specialty. Physiologists of today routinely utilize a wide spectrum of experimental animals, often selecting those which have unusual morphologies or interesting adaptations. A number of molluscs, e.g., squid and sea hares, have been used extensively for studies in neurophysiology because of the large size of their nerves. Similarly, stretch receptors from crustaceans and giant muscle fibers from barnacles offer special advantages to the investigator. Desert rodents have proven useful for experiments on kidney function and water balance. The octopus kidney also furnishes interesting material since it is inside out from most others with respect to its circulation and secretory surfaces. To emphasize further the diversity of material which animal physiologists have found useful, we could list such creatures as giraffes (blood pressure studies), seals (kidney and heat regulation), sloths (muscle physiology and temperature regulation), bats (sonar, navigation, hibernation), humming birds (metabolism), sea snakes (salt glands), silk worm moths (hormones and development), honey bees (navigation and vision), horseshoe crabs (vision) and jellyfish (primitive nervous systems) to mention only a few.

The field of physiology encompasses many different approaches and areas of study. The approach of comparative physiology is to study the responses of different animals in order to determine central mechanisms of function or to discover new solutions for common biological problems. The cell physiologists, or general physiologists, concentrate their efforts on similar problems involving cells or cell products. If the work is performed primarily at the subcellular or the molecular level, it is generally called molecular biology or biochemistry. Regardless of the level at which the work is done, if physical techniques are applied to the study of biology, the work is generally classed as biophysics. Within these broad categories, a number of subdivisions have emerged, many of which are based on the study of individual organ systems. For example, we could mention here endocrinology, renal, respiration, and circulation physiology and neurophysiology. Some subdisciplines of physiology may encompass several fields of biology with the goal of understanding some specific principle of biology. Students of physiological ecology, for example, might utilize a number of approaches in studying the short term responses or the long term adaptations of animals which occupy different environments. Their approach is even broader than that of most physiologists because it includes measurements of environmental variables as well as the responses of the organs and tissues of the animal under investigation. Although they are concerned mainly with the physiological problems of animals occupying contrasting environments such as rain forests and deserts, or freshwater and the ocean, they must also be aware of the evolution of the species they are studying and the related geologic history of the area. Classically, physiologists were not particularly concerned with the genetic basis of form and function, so this is a relatively new and fruitful approach.

Another area of research is the investigation of the processes of aging. The physiology of an animal changes continuously and often appreciably during the course of development. The advances in medicine during the past two centuries alone have lengthened man's average lifespan by almost a hundred per cent. It is not surprising, therefore, that research into the problems of senescence or aging has become important for man. Whether we work with a dog or a human, with a fly or a crustacean, we must ask ourselves how old the animal is, and how age might affect our results.

As a final example, we include also among the physiologists those who study the intriguing problems of animal migration, navigation and the biological sense of time, i.e., the biological clock. These studies, too, have become increasingly significant for man, because in our modern age of rapid travel and space exploration, there is often a dissociation of the environmental cues of time, such as day length, from the basic rhythmic changes in physiology which they affect. From the preceding statements it is clear that animal physiology is a broad field, but its subdisciplines nevertheless converge on the basic goals of explaining the functional basis of form, whether it is at the biochemical, cellular or organismal level. Quite clearly too, these studies relate to man's position in nature and to his interactions with the environment.

The advent of man on earth in large numbers is changing almost every aspect of his environment. The harnessing first of the fossil fuels, then of atomic power, has given rise to extensive urban areas, transportation facilities, industry and industrial byproducts. Man maintains large populations of domestic animals and has much of the world's fertile land under cultivation. Mismanagement of these operations results in soil erosion problems and pollution of water and air, while well-meant efforts at controlling certain animals such as insects create an accumulation of generally toxic substances. Other byproducts of modern civilization which are becoming equally hazardous include radioactive wastes and poisonous fumes. Such compounds not only threaten man and his domestic animals, they also upset the natural community in unpredictable ways. Many of these difficulties arise directly from overpopulation or at least from the fact that the growth of populations is occurring at a faster pace than our technology can accommodate. Basic problems such as an adequate food supply are already so pressing that man is depleting the oceans as well as the tillable soil in an effort to feed his growing numbers. Thus the physiology of nutrition, toxicology, growth, aging and reproduction are associated not only with other aspects of biology and medicine, but also with the social and political problems of man.

In the chapters which follow, the immediate and practical relationships between physiology and man's problems will not always be quite so obvious, since our major objective is to present the basic principles of physiology. It is hoped, however, that the reader will be induced to reflect as broadly as possible on the meaning of each principle that is given. Physiology can no longer be considered as the discipline of biology that looks into the function of a particular organ system or tissue at some point in time. Instead, it properly involves the study of diverse organisms at all levels of organization, growth, development, evolution and environmental interaction.

It is difficult to emphasize the dynamic nature of the investigations relating to physiology when one is presenting the principles for the first time. We will not always be able to present the rationale for each study under discussion or the methods used to gather the data. Often, we will be confined to giving only brief summaries of the results which were concluded from large amounts of data. The reader should realize that thousands of biologists have performed millions of individual studies in order to arrive at the few basic concepts chosen for presentation. In this context, it is of interest to note that there are more physiologists engaged in research today than in all times past. This means that we must be very selective in the examples we choose because of the large amount of relevant information available. We must also attempt a balanced presentation of all the different fields of animal physiology with material that is up to date and of general interest.

SOME EXAMPLES OF OUR APPROACH

Such traditional areas as circulation, nutrition, excretion, respiration, energetics and heat regulation are included, and, in keeping with our definition of physiology, examples have been selected from a variety of forms of animals. In certain of these discussions, however, the treatment is largely theoretical, because the biological mechanisms in some cases are so uniform that they are widely applicable to many animals. This approach has been taken, for example, in discussions involving biological oxidations and to a lesser extent in presenting the physical aspects of circulation. In certain discussions, particularly those dealing with excretion, respiration, and energetics, a quantitative approach is taken because the important concepts are summarized concisely by elementary mathematics. This approach not only allows one readily to relate important parameters, it also emphasizes that physiology is a quantitative field of biology requiring accurate measurements.

Some of the chapters to follow have been concluded by a summarizing example or by one which gives an interesting solution to some particular biological problem. Ruminant digestion, for example, has been used to emphasize several principles of animal nutrition. Many ruminants, such as cattle and sheep, are able to utilize the extremely abundant cellulose of plants as a food source. Ordinarily, cellulose is not directly available to most higher animals because they are incapable of degrading it to simple sugars. We shall see, however, that ruminant animals can utilize cellulose due to the presence of a fermentation tank in the gastrointestinal tract that is filled with cellulose-degrading microorganisms. Although this seems unusual, it will be shown that almost every animal depends upon intestinal bacteria for some of its essential nutrients.

Studies on excretion and osmoregulation offer some excellent examples of physiological adaptations to certain environments. It will be shown that marine birds, and at least some marine and terrestrial reptiles, have evolved special salt glands in their heads which allow them to remain in salt and water balance even if they drink sea water. Still other animals, as different as sharks and frogs, have evolved the common mechanism of retaining urea in their tissues in sufficient amounts to prevent dehydration while living in sea water.

Every study of physiology, including the present one, offers some treatment of the effectors of locomotion, the muscles. One cannot help but admire the biological engineering that has gone into these cells. Like other tissues, they are composed of about two-thirds water, yet a strip of mammalian skeletal muscle of about one square inch in cross section can exert a tension in excess of 40 pounds. Many morphological forms and functions of muscle are known from the animal kingdom, ranging from those involved in insect flight to those which close the shells of clams. Some of these specialized muscles will be described, particularly with reference to the activating mechanisms which provide for wide gradations of strength and speed of contraction. In addition, a most highly evolved form of muscle, the electric organs of certain fish, is described briefly. One of the most interesting aspects of the whole topic is that these divergent morphologies have evolved and their functions are accomplished in spite of the fact that the contractile proteins of all muscles are very similar.

Perhaps the most spectacular examples of current studies in cellular and comparative physiology are to be found in the work on receptors and nervous systems. Animals have evolved receptors which sense such minute physical and chemical changes in the environment that they approach the theoretical limits. For example, a rod receptor in the human eye responds when only a single molecule of retinal pigment absorbs one minimal energy unit of light (a single quantum). Equally impressive is the fact that the human ear is responsive to sound waves which displace the eardrum by only about 10^{-9} centimeters (four ten-billionths of an inch). There are a number of animals, e.g., the insectivorous bats, that have incorporated this remarkable auditory sensitivity into a sonar system for navigation. They receive and interpret the echoes of their own cries returning from objects in the environment. The accuracy of this process in locating and detecting movements of objects in the environment is truly phenomenal, in fact it approaches the precision of vision. We shall find that not all animals utilize the conventional senses of sight, hearing and smell to assess the environment around them. The pit viper snakes, for example, "see" in the dark by using their facial pits to sense the infrared radiation emitted by their prey. Fish which possess the electric organs mentioned above obtain their major knowledge of the environment by interpreting the distortions of electrical pulses which they themselves produce. We will also consider the process by which receptor information is rapidly transferred from nerve cell to nerve cell in the central nervous system. We will find that such integration is accomplished almost instantaneously, in part by virtue of the startling speeds of conduction of the long nerve branches. The larger nerves in the mammalian spinal cord, for instance, conduct impulses at speeds which could traverse a football field in one second.

Finally, we will consider the integration of such processes as growth and development, which are directed by the chemical messages of hormones and pheromones. We will see, for instance, how a few molecules of these important compounds can change the whole course of development and growth, or the behavior of an animal, if they are applied under the proper circumstances.

All of these phenomena and many others make up the broad science of animal physiology. It is an exciting area of biology which is changing rapidly. As new data accumulate, the theories as well as the experimental approaches are undergoing an evolution. The field is in fact different from that of only a decade ago, not only because of new information, but because we are interpreting the older information in different ways. It is understood that the numerous aspects of the science of living animals cannot be put into proper perspective when taking the point of view offered by any single discipline. But the approach offered here for animal physiology should serve its purpose when considered as one part of an introduction to biology.

CHAPTER 2

Body fluids and circulation

CELL MEMBRANES AND PERMEABILITY

Consider for a moment a single animal cell. Within it lies all the machinery necessary for growth, repair and reproduction. But the cell is not a self-sufficient entity. Like a machine it requires an external source of raw materials and energy. Its metabolism results in the formation of waste materials that are toxic if permitted to accumulate. Thus the composition of the fluid immediately outside the cell membrane is of major importance to the normal functions of cells and tissues. This reservoir not only furnishes the nutrients for the tissues, it also receives and removes the byproducts of metabolism. Our purpose here will be to examine some of the chemical and physical interactions which occur between cells and surrounding fluids. Interaction is an appropriate term since the cell not only acts on the fluids, but constituents of the fluid alter the responses of the cell.

The major structure which determines the entrance and exit of materials into and out of a cell is the plasma membrane, a highly organized complex of lipid (fat) and protein. The membrane may contain pores of various size which permit or limit the passage of chemicals across the cell surface. The passage of particles across the cell surface depends to some extent upon their solubility in the chemicals composing the membrane itself. Thus fat-soluble substances may preferentially pass through the fatty areas of the membrane while ionized (electrically charged) substances enter or leave by way of the protein patches and pores. In addition, there are specific "pumps" which actively introduce or extrude certain substances into or out of the cell. Finally, the surface membrane also generally possesses an electrical charge between the inside and outside, which either repels or attracts ionized chemicals in the environment. The *direction* of net movement of substances across the membrane is determined largely by the concentration differences across the membrane, the voltage gradient and the activities of the various pumps. We will next illustrate and describe briefly each of these factors that determine overall permeability.

The simplest driving force for the movement of materials across a cell membrane is the concentration difference. In any solution, the molecules of both solvent and solute are in constant motion because of their kinetic energies. Individual molecules thus collide and recoil from each other without loss of energy. The probability that a given molecule or ion will collide with one of its own kind depends upon how many such molecules or ions there are per unit volume. Repeated collisions between molecules of a certain kind tend to disperse them from regions of high concentration (frequent collisions) to regions of lower concentration (few collisions). The resulting movement of a molecular species is called *diffusion*. Diffusion continues until equilibrium is reached, that is, the concentration of molecules is the same throughout the available space. Consider the diagram of Fig. 2-1. Assume that two compartments of equal size are divided by a partition which completely blocks diffusion. Following the removal of the barrier, diffusion begins rapidly because the concentration difference is initially high. While the dissolved substance diffuses from its area of higher concentration (left to right), water is also diffusing from its area of high concentration (right to left). As time passes (time = 1, = 2 and = 3) the solute eventually becomes evenly distributed throughout the entire volume. The graphs of concentration *versus* distance describe the process. The slope of the line drawn tangential to the curve represents the *gradient for diffusion* (change in concentration per unit distance). The steeper the slope, the more rapid the diffusion.

Next, let us consider the effect of placing between the two compartments a cell membrane which is permeable to the diffusing substance (Fig. 2-2). The gradient across the membrane is at first very high since the concentration difference is great and the distance is very short (the thickness of the membrane). Diffusion proceeds as before, but much more slowly since the membrane retards the process. The ease with which a specific substance crosses the membrane is given by the *diffusion constant*. The net movement of a substance is thus dependent upon two factors, its diffusion constant and the gradient. In the case

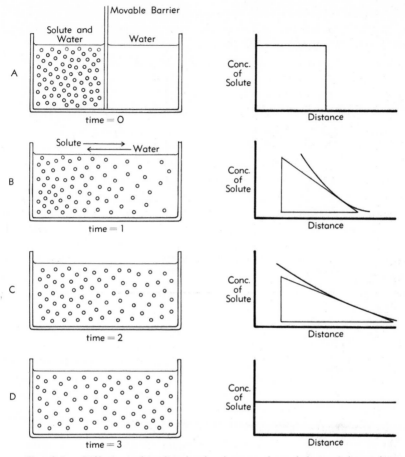

Fig. 2-1. Diffusion of a dissolved substance from left to right and the diffusion of water from right to left. The corresponding graphs at the right show the concentration of the solute at various distances along the container as diffusion proceeds from time = 0 to time = 3. The slope of the line at any point indicates the gradient (change in concentration with distance).

of very permeable membranes, such as those which line the capillaries, the rate of diffusion is high enough to insure virtually equal concentrations of many substances across the walls, particularly at low blood flow rates. Adequate gas diffusion in the lungs, for example, is generally accomplished with low gradients since the diffusion constant is high. Equilibrium is reached between alveolar gas and blood gas in a matter of less than one second, which constitutes the exposure time of red blood cells

9

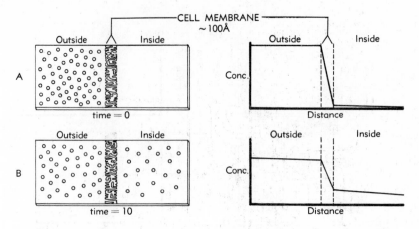

Fig. 2-2. The effect of placing a barrier such as a cell membrane in the diffusion path. The gradient may be very high since the diffusion distance, i.e., the thickness of the cell membrane, is only about 100 Angstroms (1 Angstrom = one hundred-millionth of a centimeter). Diffusion rate is slowed such that at time = 10 (as compared to time = 3 in Fig. 2-1) equilibrium has not yet been reached. See text.

in alveolar capillaries. The maintenance of maximal diffusion rates, however, often requires that the diffusing substance be replenished on the original side of the exchange membrane. Otherwise the concentration on that side would drop thus making the diffusion gradient across the membrane less steep and lowering the rate of diffusion. This problem will be discussed in more detail in later chapters.

As noted above, the complex molecular organization of cell membranes contributes to their permeability properties. Some of these functional properties are presented diagrammatically in Fig. 2-3. The permeability of most cells to potassium ions (K^+) is generally higher than to sodium (Na^+). The diameter of a hydrated K^+ ion is about 3.96 Angstroms (A) while that of Na^+ is near 5.12 A. Pore size alone could be expected therefore to limit Na^+ permeability under some conditions.

The relative importance of transmembrane voltage and electrical charges on the pores may be seen when one compares the permeability of an ionized (amino acids, inorganic compounds, e.g.) and a non-ionized substance (fats, carbohydrates, e.g.). Since non-ionized materials are unaffected by membrane charge, they are often more permeable than ionized substances. This is logical since the absence of ionic charges eliminates the possibility of attraction or repulsion between the permeating molecule and those which compose the membrane. Lipid solubility

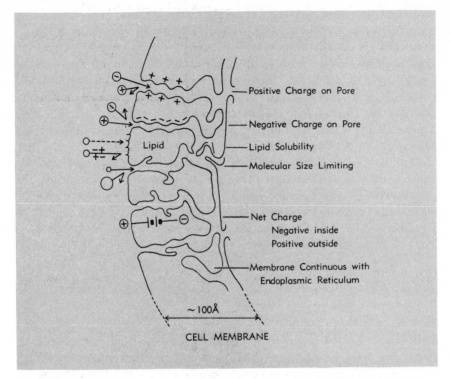

Fig. 2-3. Some local properties of cell membranes which influence permeability (see text).

also favors passage since the membrane contains considerable amounts of fat. Alternatively, an ionized substance of low fat solubility may show a high permeability if it is driven by the voltage gradient of the transmembrane potential or if it is actively transported.

The ability to effect active transport, that is, to move molecules or ions against a concentration or voltage gradient, is a property of all cell membranes. We are not yet able to describe these processes in detail, because we do not know the components nor the mode of operation of any active transport pump. However, the diagram in Fig. 2-4, conveys some idea of the process. Here, the active transport of the negatively charged substance (Z^-) is occurring against a concentration gradient (concentration of (Z^-) is higher inside) and against a voltage gradient (cell interior negatively charged). It is assumed that several "carrier molecules", designated as (Y) in the diagram, are needed for the process. The critical factors of direction of movement and molecular specificity are somehow introduced by the carrier (Y). Thus, this hypothetical pump probably will move only (Z$^-$) molecules, and only in an inward direction. It is an equally important characteristic of membrane pumps that they require energy, presumably derived from adenosine triphosphate (ATP). ATP is produced largely by aerobic respiration. Removal of the oxygen supply, lowering of the temperature, or addition of respiratory poisons will slow down or abolish respiration. Since these treatments have similar effects on active transport, it is inferred that this process runs on the energy of ATP molecules.

Another means of achieving transport of certain substances across cell membranes is pinocytosis (Fig. 2-4), a movement somewhat like the engulfment process (phagocytosis) by which amoeboid cells feed. The "drinking" of fluids by pinocytosis is known to result in the uptake of large molecules, such as proteins, which would otherwise fail to cross the cell membrane. Although the number of cell types which undergo

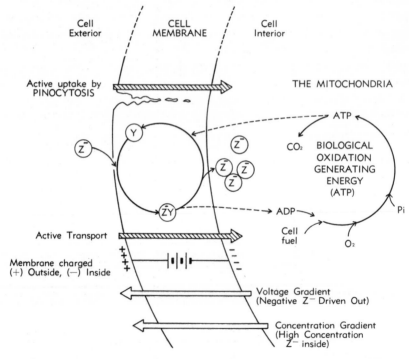

Fig. 2-4. A schematic representation of active transport as it might occur in opposing both voltage and concentration gradients. The energy required for the process is derived from biological oxidations. A second type of active transport called pinocytosis is also shown.

pinocytosis is not known, the process may be an important one in many of the less specialized cells of multicellular organisms.

BODY FLUIDS

Among the consequences of these membrane functions is the establishment of fluids of rather strict composition that are distributed inside or outside of cells in an equally specific way. In the next few pages we will focus our attention on the composition of body fluids and on their distribution within a living animal.

It is important to emphasize at the outset the important role of water in the makeup of living organisms. In addition to being a general solvent for biological compounds, water has several other useful properties. For example, a considerable amount of heat must be added to water to raise its temperature. This is important in maintaining the relatively constant temperatures required by living systems. Also, the absorption of relatively large amounts of heat is needed to convert liquid water to vapor. As a result of this property, the vaporization of the water as perspiration can provide an effective means of cooling the body. In addition, water itself enters many fundamental chemical reactions of living organisms. During digestion, for example, foodstuffs are usually split into smaller units by the incorporation of water (the process of hydrolysis). On the other hand many of the synthesizing reactions of tissues, such as those giving rise to proteins and carbohydrates, as well as the general processes of biological oxidation, release water into the cellular fluids.

An average adult mammal contains between 55% and 65% water by weight; in the newborn, it is near 75%. Variations in the water content of individual organs of a typical mammal are shown in Table 2-1.

TABLE 2-1

Water Content of the Tissues of a Rabbit
Given as Per Cent Water by Weight

Brain	80%
Small Intestine	80%
Heart	78%
Muscle	77%
Bone	40%
Hair	12%

The distribution of these fluids into "spaces" is shown in the flow diagram below. These figures are based on the assumption that the total body water is 58% of the body weight, and the organism is a human weighing 70 kilograms (1 kilogram = 2.204 lb). A comparable percentage distribution would be found in other mammals.

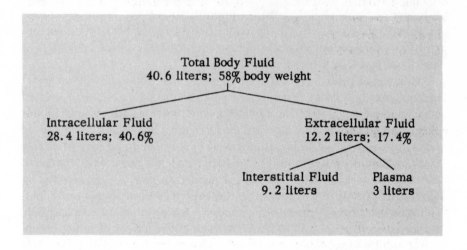

Although we speak of "fluid compartments" or "spaces" such as intra- or extracellular fluid, these are actually only mental images, since the body fluids and their chemical contents are continually exchanging among the spaces. Generally, the amount entering is equal to the amount leaving at any one time; a condition referred to as a "steady state." The volumes are real in the sense that they are measurable, through the use of substances which, for permeability reasons, are confined to a certain compartment.

The measurement of body spaces is done routinely by *dilution techniques* and by *difference* (subtraction from other known volumes). Plasma volume may be measured by dilution techniques. A *known quantity* of a non-toxic dye such as Evans blue, which attaches to plasma proteins, is injected into the circulatory system. Since proteins move slowly across capillary walls and since they are not removed by the kidney, the dye is confined to the circulation long enough to insure complete mixing (about 10 to 20 minutes in mammals). A sample of blood is then withdrawn and the concentration of dye is determined for the sample. Plasma volume may then by calculated as follows:

$$\text{mg injected}/(\text{mg/ml}) \text{ in plasma} = \text{volume of plasma (ml)} \quad (1)$$

Total blood volume may be estimated next if the relative volumes of red cells and plasma are known. This requires a second measurement, known as the *hematocrit*. A blood sample is placed in a parallel-walled capillary tube. The tube is centrifuged to separate the cells from the plasma. The percentage of the blood volume comprised of red cells is calculated from the ratio of the length of the column of RBC's to the length of the entire column. This figure is the hematocrit. Since the plasma portion of the blood is equal to 100% minus the per cent of RBC's, a proportion may be set up:

$$\frac{\text{Blood volume}}{100} = \frac{\text{Plasma volume}}{100 - \text{hematocrit}}$$

which can be converted to the following equation from which total blood volume is calculated:

$$\text{Blood volume} = \text{Plasma volume} \times \frac{100}{100 - \text{hematocrit}} \qquad (2)$$

Typical hematocrit values range from about 40% to 45%. If the plasma volume is 3 liters and the hematocrit is 45, the total blood volume may be calculated, using the above formula (2), to be 5.45 liters.

The dilution technique may also be used to determine the volume of total body water and the volume of extracellular fluid. In the first instance a substance which exchanges readily with all body water is injected. Such a substance is D_2O (D is deuterium, or heavy hydrogen, a non-radioactive isotope). In the second instance substances are used which pass readily through capillaries, but fail to penetrate cells. Sodium and thiocyanate ions and the polysaccharide inulin satisfy these requirements.

The difference method may be used to determine the intracellular volume and the interstitial (between the cells) volume if the previous determinations have been made:

$$\begin{bmatrix} \text{Intracellular} \\ \text{volume} \\ \text{28.4 liters} \end{bmatrix} = \begin{bmatrix} \text{total fluid} \\ \text{volume} \\ \text{40.6 liters} \end{bmatrix} - \begin{bmatrix} \text{extracellular} \\ \text{fluid volume} \\ \text{12.2 liters} \end{bmatrix} \qquad (3)$$

$$\begin{bmatrix} \text{Interstitial} \\ \text{volume} \\ \text{9.2 liters} \end{bmatrix} = \begin{bmatrix} \text{extracellular} \\ \text{volume} \\ \text{12.2 liters} \end{bmatrix} - \begin{bmatrix} \text{plasma volume} \\ \text{3 liters} \end{bmatrix} \qquad (4)$$

In spite of its relatively small volume, the plasma compartment assumes a major role in fluid exchange and regulation. It is the only volume in which rapid circulation is maintained. It is forced through the capillary beds which provide a highly permeable and expansive surface for exchange of fluid and constituents with the interstitial fluid. Interstitial fluid, on the other hand, does not circulate. Instead it is a highly dispersed pool in which all of the cells of the body are bathed directly. It should be noted, that more than two-thirds of all the fluid in the body is inside the cells and that this intracellular fluid is most remote from the circulation, being buffered, as it were, by the cell membranes and extracellular spaces.

COMPOSITION OF BODY FLUIDS

Some of the chemical constituents of plasma, interstitial fluid and cellular fluid are summarized in Table 2-2 below.

TABLE 2-2

Chemical Composition of Body Fluids

Plasma	Interstitial Fluid	Intracellular Fluid
	(Major Constituents)	
Na^+	Na^+	K^+, Mg^{++}
Cl^-, HCO_3^-, Protein	Cl^-, HCO_3^-	$PO_4^=$, $SO_4^=$, Protein
	(Minor Constituents)	
K^+, Ca^{++}, Mg^{++}	K^+, Ca^{++}, Mg^{++}	Na^+, Ca^{++}
$HPO_4^=$, SO_4	$HPO_4^=$, $SO_4^=$	HCO_3^-
Amino acids, fats	Amino acids, fats, proteins	Amino acids, fats
Sugars, fatty acids	Sugars, fatty acids	Sugars, fatty acids
Organic acids	Organic acids	Organic acids
Hormones, vitamins	Hormones, vitamins	Hormones, vitamins

The major extracellular cation ($+$ charged ion) is sodium, while the major intracellular cation is potassium. Chloride and bicarbonate are the major anions ($-$ charged ions) outside of cells, while phosphate and sulfate ions and proteins are largely intracellular. It should be pointed out, too, that interstitial fluid is very similar in composition to plasma with the exception of proteins, which are largely confined to the plasma. This similarity reflects the high permeability of the capillary walls. Proteins, however, of molecular weight above 60,000 fail to pass through the capillary membrane pores. The major plasma proteins are larger than this and so are confined to the plasma. The composition of body fluids, as noted above, is dependent upon the permeabilities of the capillary walls and cell membranes as well as the activities of the cellular pumps and cellular utilization and excretion. The regulation of fluid constituents will be considered in later discussions.

CIRCULATION

Blood flow is governed by the same physical factors that determine fluid movement in any system, i.e., the relationships between pressure and resistance. The individual factors which describe pressure and resistance in circulatory systems are, however, somewhat more complex than those for a rigid system of tubes. For example, the circulatory system contains elastic vessels which not only vary in diameter but taper and divide in various ways. The smallest of the vessels, the capillaries, may passively collapse and require considerable pressure to open. The reservoirs of the circulation, such as those of the liver or the capillary beds of the skin and intestine, vary considerably in volume. Finally, blood flow is at times turbulent and at other times laminar (smooth). These and other considerations contribute to the overall relationship:

$$\text{Blood Flow} = \frac{\text{Pressure drop } (\Delta P)}{\text{Resistance } (R)} \tag{5}$$

From elementary physics we recall that fluid will not flow in a vessel unless a pressure difference exists between two points. This pressure drop, which we will represent by the symbol ΔP, is brought about in the circulatory system by three factors; a pump, resistance, and some appropriately located valves. Since pressure is exerted by the heart working against resistance, our major concern therefore is to describe the factors which contribute to resistance, with particular attention to those which are under control of the organism.

The major factors controlling resistance in circulatory systems are the radius of the vessel (r), its length (l) and fluid viscosity (η). As blood flows through a vessel it encounters the shearing forces of the surrounding fluid layers and the friction of the stationary walls. If the walls are parallel, each unit of vessel length will impose an equal unit of resistance from its wall surface. In short, the total resistance is proportional to total length (l). The relative volume-to-surface ratio of vessels changes greatly with small changes in radius. As vessels become larger, relatively more blood flows through them without meeting the shearing forces near the walls or the direct friction of the walls themselves. Consequently, resistance is inversely proportional to the fourth power of the vessel radius (1 r⁴). Finally, resistance is directly proportional to viscosity (η). In other words, more pressure is needed to force a syrupy liquid through a tube than is needed for a thin watery one. In blood, viscosity is determined largely by red cell and protein content. The three factors affecting resistance may be summarized in the general expression:

$$\text{Resistance (R)} = (1) \cdot (\eta) \cdot 1/r^4 \tag{6}$$

and since blood flow is given by the expression,

$$\text{B.F.} = \frac{\Delta P}{R} \tag{5}$$

we may substitute the values for (R) in equation (6) into equation (5) and obtain equation (7), the formula of Poiseuille:

$$\text{B.F.} = \frac{\Delta P}{(1) \cdot (\eta) \cdot (1/r^4)} \tag{7}$$

There are no reflex mechanisms in animals for significantly changing vessel length (1) or blood viscosity (η). Although these factors are important, they must be considered as relatively constant contributors to resistance. The only factors, therefore, that are under the control of the organism are pressure and vessel diameter. Due to the dependence of resistance upon the fourth power of the vessel radius, relatively small changes in vessel size lead to large changes in blood flow. In the vertebrates, the arterioles, which lie immediately in front of the capillary bed, are supplied with a layer of smooth muscle that is innervated mainly from the sympathetic nervous system. Changes in tension in this muscle coat alter the radius and thus the resistance to flow. The arterioles are of great importance in the control of resistance; almost half the total pressure drop between the aorta and the vena cava occurs in these vessels. In addition, the arteriolar pressures directly control capillary flow, and as will be shown below, capillary perfusion rate determines the rate of exchange of materials between plasma and interstitial fluid.

THE HEART AS A PUMP

The initial source of pressure in the circulation is the heart. Since the heart is a pulsing pump as opposed to a continuous one, its operation consists of a series of contractions or strokes, each of which ejects a quantity of blood (stroke volume). The *output* of the heart can be expressed as volume pumped per minute:

$$(\text{ml/stroke}) \times (\text{strokes/minute}) = \text{Cardiac output (ml/min)} \quad (8)$$

Control of pump performance may therefore involve stroke volume or rate (strokes/min) or both. In man, cardiac output can range from about 5 liters per minute at rest, to slightly more than 20 liters per minute during strenuous exercise. The relative contribution of rate change and stroke volume change to the output is shown in Table 2-3.

TABLE 2-3

Cardiac Output in Man at Rest and During Exercise

	Rest	Exercise
Rate	— 70/min	200/min
Stroke volume	— 72 ml	100 ml
Cardiac output	— 5l/min	20 L/min

The increase in stroke volume is limited in part by the filling process at high heart rates. Since the circulation of the blood is a closed system, the cardiac output equals the venous return (Fig. 2-5). More specifically, since the heart is in fact two pumps in series, the cardiac output to the lungs (pulmonary cardiac output) equals the systemic venous return and systemic cardiac output equals pulmonary venous return. The pressure gradient in the pulmonary circuit is much less than that of the systemic circuit, but equal cardiac output is possible from both, however, since resistance is proportionately larger in the high pressure systemic circuit and lower in the low pressure pulmonary circuit.

The hearts of animals in general are spontaneously active. This means that the excitability and rhythmicity of contraction reside within the heart itself. Vertebrate hearts are said to be "myogenic" since the muscle tissue is spontaneously excitable. In many invertebrate animals the hearts are "neurogenic" meaning that they are activated and paced by local spontaneously active neurons within the heart. If an isolated strip of auricle or ventricle from a vertebrate heart is placed in a balanced salt solution, it will continue to contract for some time. Although spontaneous excitability is a property of all parts of the heart muscle, the rate of contraction of an isolated auricle (atrium) is faster than that of a ven-

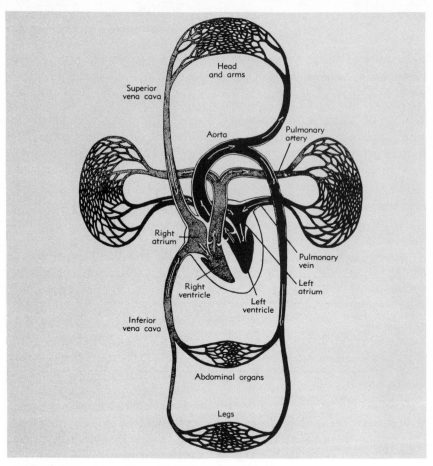

Fig. 2-5. A schematic representation of the major morphological features of a mammalian circulatory system. The course of the circulating blood is shown by the arrows. Blood leaving the left ventricle enters the aorta and courses to the systemic blood vessels. It returns to the right auricle (= atrium) from which it passes into the right ventricle and then to the pulmonary circulation. This route also represents the direction of pressure drop in the system. The networks of smaller vessels, shown here in a very abbreviated form, represent the extensive capillary beds of various tissues and organs. It is at these sites that exchange occurs between substances in the blood and in the tissues.

The darker portions of the system indicate oxygenated blood, while the lighter portions represent blood that is partly depleted as a result of oxygen utilization by the tissues. Carbon dioxide, not shown, is released by the tissues and is carried to the lungs where it is expelled. Note that systemic venous return supplies the blood for the pulmonary circulation. The heart therefore is actually two pumps in series. (From Whaley, G. W. et al., **Principles of Biology,** Harper and Row, New York, 3rd. ed., 1964, as redrawn from C. J. Wiggers, "The Heart." Scientific American, May, 1957.)

tricle. A small patch of mammalian right auricle, located near the entrance of the vena cava, functions as the pacemaker, since it has the fastest rhythm of any heart tissue and imposes this rate on the remaining parts of the heart. The pacemaker tissue is called the sinoauricular node (S-A node). The sinus venosus of fish and amphibian hearts, which functions as the pacemaker in these groups, is homologous to it.

It is possible for a wave of excitation to spread from the pacemaker site through the muscle to all parts of the heart, producing a sequential contraction first of the auricles, then of the ventricles. These are essentially the events of the cardiac cycle of the primitive vertebrate hearts. In the birds and mammals, however, a special *conducting system* has evolved from muscle tissue which insures an efficient rate, extent and sequence of excitation. The conducting tissue includes the atrioventricular bundle (A-V bundle) which courses through the septum which separates the ventricular chambers (Fig. 2-6A). In the mammalian heart, the excitation from the S-A node spreads over the auricles in such a way that both contract essentially simultaneously to expel their contents into the ventricular chambers. One-way valves are present in the large veins of the heart which prevent back flow as auricular pressure rises. Pressure in the auricles forces the valves situated between the auricles and ventricles to open, thus causing the ventricles to fill. At this point there

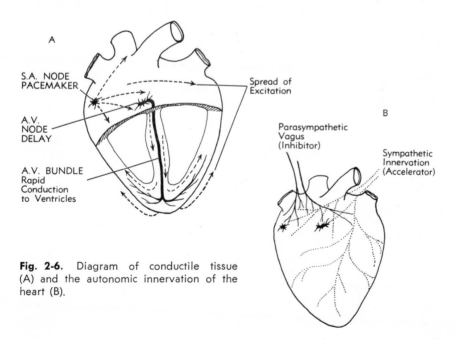

Fig. 2-6. Diagram of conductile tissue (A) and the autonomic innervation of the heart (B).

is a slight delay in conduction from the A-V node to the A-V bundle; this insures adequate filling time for the ventricles. Conduction then proceeds rapidly in the A-V bundle and out to both ventricles, resulting in their simultaneous contraction. As ventricular pressure rises, the valves to the auricles close and those to the pulmonary and systemic arteries open. Once the ventricular contents are expelled, the arterial valves close, thereby retaining the pressure in the arteries.

From the time blood leaves the heart until it returns to it, several drops in pressure occur. During ventricular contraction, the pressure in the systemic arteries, the *systolic pressure*, reaches about 120 mm Hg. (Since the body is ordinarily at atmospheric pressure of about 760 mm Hg, the pressures developed inside the circulatory system are given in millimeters of mercury above atmospheric.) As the blood flows through the arterial tree to the capillaries and veins, however, the pressure in the aorta drops to its lowest value, the *diastolic pressure*, of about 80 mm Hg. The fluctuation within the arterial system which accompanies heart contractions then amounts to about 40 mm Hg (120-80). This value is known as the *pulse pressure*. At other points in the systemic circuit, blood pressures become progressively lower. Because of the high resistance that is imposed, much of this pressure drop occurs at the level of the arterioles. The pressure in the capillaries is near 35 mm Hg, but diminishes to about 15 mm Hg in the small veins and finally reaches near zero (= atmospheric pressure) in the vena cava.

EXCHANGES IN THE CAPILLARIES: ORIGIN OF LYMPH

Capillaries allow relatively unimpeded movement of small molecules across their walls as long as appropriate concentration gradients exist. Since neither active transport nor a voltage gradient is involved in the passage of substances across capillary walls, diffusion alone accounts for most of the exchange. In our general discussion of permeability we noted that diffusion rate is dependent on two factors, the diffusion constant and the concentration gradient. However, the total amount of diffusion that occurs can be greatly enhanced by increasing the surface area available for diffusion. The capillary beds of mammalian circulatory systems are wonderfully adapted in this respect.

Capillaries are the smallest blood vessels. In fact they are on the average only slightly larger in diameter than red cells, or about 8-10 microns (1 micron = one thousandth of a millimeter). The walls are a single cell thick and contain no muscles; as a result, capillary diameter is largely a function of local blood pressure. Estimates of average lengths of capillaries range from 0.4 to 0.7 mm. August Krogh, who contributed much to our knowledge of capillaries, has provided the following figures for capillary density and surface area in dog skeletal muscle. Capillaries here number about 2600 per mm^2 of muscle, providing a diffusion surface of nearly 590 cm^2 per cubic centimeter of tissue! This density of vessels also insures that individual cells are rarely more distant than 50 microns from a capillary.

In addition to diffusion, the capillary exchange processes include fluid filtration and reabsorption. Osmotic pressure plays a direct role in the fluid exchanges in capillaries; therefore, let us digress and examine a simple model of the process before proceeding to the living system. Osmosis, and the development of osmotic pressure, represents in essence a special case of diffusion. In our model (Fig. 2-7) a dilute protein solution, similar to plasma, is placed inside a thistle tube covered

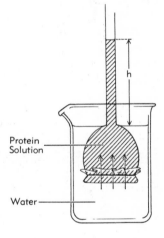

Fig. 2-7. Diagram illustrating the development of osmotic pressure. A solution of non-diffusible substance is separated by a thin cellophane membrane from a solution of pure water. Since only water can cross the membrane, it diffuses into the protein solution until the pressure exerted by the column in the stem (h) equals the osmotic pressure of the protein solution. The pressure developed is proportional to the number of non-diffusible molecules present.

with cellophane. The cellophane, like a capillary wall, will allow small molecules such as salts and water to pass through, but will retard greatly the passage of large molecules. The tube is next inverted and placed in a vessel of distilled water with the level of the inner solution even with the level of the distilled water outside. When the tube is immersed, the water, which is more concentrated outside than inside, begins to *diffuse* inward, causing the fluid level in the stem to rise. This kind of diffusion through a membrane is called *osmosis*. Eventually, the rising column of fluid everts a downward pressure that causes osmosis to stop. This pressure is equal to the osmotic pressure of the protein solution. If we put into

the tube a more concentrated protein solution, that is, one of higher osmotic pressure, the height (h) and the pressure of the column will increase in proportion to the number of protein molecules present. Suppose
we now apply some additional pressure downward to the column by
means of a pump. We could then force some water from the protein solution into the outside vessel. Similar opposing forces, that is, blood pressure and osmotic pressure, operate very much in this way in the capillary
(Fig. 2-8). The blood pressure at the arteriolar end of a capillary is
about 35 mm Hg. The difference in pressure not only propels blood along
the vessel, but also tends to drive some fluid out through the walls into
the interstitial space. On the other hand, the osmotic pressure exerted
by the plasma proteins within the capillaries is about 25 mm Hg (Fig.
2-8), and this force tends to draw fluids into the capillary. Since the
osmotic pressure (O.P.) of the proteins does not equal the blood pressure, some fluid is filtered out of the capillary at the arterial end. As
the blood pressure falls near the center of the capillary, the O.P. equals
the blood pressure so that no net fluid movement occurs. Here, and
at other points along the capillary, diffusion of small solute molecules
is occurring, however, since it is driven only by concentration differences.
At the venous end of the capillary, the O.P. exceeds the blood pressure
causing interstitial fluid to be drawn back into the vessel. Any excess

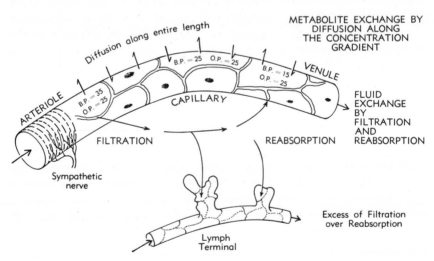

Fig. 2-8. Fluid and metabolite exchanges at the level of the capillaries.
The excess fluid that is filtered but not reabsorbed into the capillary is
carried back to the circulation via the lymphatic vessels. Note that the
metabolite exchange occurs primarily by diffusion and is largely independent of fluid exchange.

fluid which is filtered but not reabsorbed by the capillaries is carried away by the lymphatic vessels (Fig. 2-8). In humans there is a filtration out of the arterial end of all the capillaries in the body of about 800-1000 ml/hr. Approximately 700-900 ml of this filtrate returns directly to the capillary at the venous end. The remaining 100 ml/hr returns to the circulation *via* the lymphatic vessels. This fluid exchange is subsidiary to the concurrent diffusion process, however, which results in exchange of small metabolite molecules. In general, the fuels and raw materials for synthetic activities move out of the capillaries toward the tissues, while the byproducts of cell metabolism tend to move from the tissues into the capillaries, each substance moving as directed by its concentration gradient.

The permeability of the capillary wall to metabolites is sufficiently great that *diffusion equilibrium* may virtually be reached at *slow* blood flow rates. That is, if the flow is slow enough to allow considerable diffusion time, the concentrations of the diffusible substances on the two sides of the capillary wall can become essentially equal. The realization of diffusion equilibrium may in fact limit the quantity of material which can cross the capillary walls. If blood flow is high, and equilibrium is *almost* achieved, the maximum quantity of diffusing substance can be transported. This is of particular importance in the transfer of highly diffusible materials such as the respiratory gases, O_2 and CO_2. Rapid capillary blood flow is therefore important in maintaining a favorable gradient by replenishing the exchange sites on the internal walls of the capillary.

Capillaries do not remain open continually, in fact as many as half of them may be closed at any one time. This appears to result from a property of the smooth muscles of the arterioles. Like many other smooth muscles, those of the arterioles are spontaneously active and undergo slow contraction and relaxation cycles about every 20 seconds. Since these cycles of contraction are not synchronized in all the capillaries of the body, some vessels are open while others are closed. Superimposed upon this spontaneous activity are two control systems, a local chemical control and a nervous control. If the blood supply to a segment of tissue is occluded for a short time, or if a particular muscle is called upon to exert great force, the local concentration of O_2 diminishes and that of CO_2 increases. The concentrations of lactic acid and other metabolites may also increase. By an unexplained means, these chemical changes lead to a relaxation of precapillary sphincters and a corresponding increase in blood flow. Such a process of local control of tissue perfusion has been termed "reactive hyperemia." The major nerve supply to the arteriolar smooth muscles is derived from the sympathetic branch of the autonomic nervous system. In most tissues, sympathetic activity causes arteriolar constriction and a diminished capillary pressure and flow. In heart and skeletal muscle, however, sympathetic activation produces a relaxation of precapillary sphincters and thus an increased blood flow. Control by local tissue chemicals may be the more important of the two mechanisms since chemical regulation allows the blood flow to be altered locally as the conditions demand.

LYMPHATIC SYSTEM

The lymphatic systems of mammals, like their circulatory systems, are distributed throughout the body. Morphologically, the smaller lymph vessels resemble capillaries since their walls are made up of a single layer of cells. The vessels differ from capillaries, however, since they end blindly in the interstitial spaces. In mammals, there are no lymphatic hearts, and even the main lymph vessels are without muscular elements in their walls. Both the veins and the major lymphatic vessels have one-way valves along their length which direct the fluid flow toward the heart. Lymph is propelled almost entirely by the pumping action of the general body musculature. Since a relatively small pressure drop is present in veins, blood movement is augmented by skeletal muscle contractions here as well. The lymphatics ultimately drain into the large veins near the heart.

REGULATION OF THE CIRCULATORY SYSTEM

We have seen that mechanisms are provided for changing total circulation by varying peripheral resistance and cardiac output. It is important to remember, too, that limits are set on both these parameters. The animal, for example, cannot afford to overwork the heart or it will fail, and excessive pressures cannot be allowed to develop in the vessels or they may break. Blood flow, even under normal conditions, may limit the rate of metabolism of an animal, particularly during exercise when oxygen and nutrients are needed most.

In vertebrate animals the hierarchy of control for the circulation begins with the vasomotor center of the brain. This center essentially directs the activity of those parts of the autonomic nervous system which innervate the blood vessels and the heart. Like other control centers, it must be provided with information, on the basis of which appropriate adjustments can be made. This information is obtained continually from numerous receptors strategically located either within the circulatory system or in other parts of the body. For example, information on the arterial pressure is furnished by stretch-sensitive receptors in some of the large arteries, while information on the chemical condition of local brain tissues is directly available. During exercise, data on movements of the muscles and joints are also conveyed to the vasomotor center. In summary, the vasomotor center activates the autonomic motor fibers to speed or slow the heart and to alter blood vessel diameter (resistance) in accordance with the information that is being received concerning the status of the overall circulation and the needs of various tissues.

REFERENCES

BOURNE, GEOFFREY H., *Division of Labor in Cells.* New York: Academic Press, 1962. Ch. 2.

GIESE, ARTHUR C., *Cell Physiology,* 2nd ed. Philadelphia: W. B. Saunders Co., 1962. Ch. 2, 3, 5, 11, 12, 13.

GUYTON, A. C., *Textbook of Medical Physiology,* 2nd ed. Philadelphia: W. B. Saunders Co., 1961. Ch. 3, 4, 5, 6, 21, 25, 26, 32.

PROSSER, C. L., and BROWN, F. A. JR., *Comparative Animal Physiology,* 2nd ed. Philadelphia: W. B. Saunders Co., 1961. Ch. 3, 13.

RUCH, T. C., and FULTON, J. F., (eds.), *Medical Physiology and Biophysics,* 18th ed. Philadelphia: W. B. Saunders Co., 1960. Ch. 24, 29, 30.

WIGGERS, CARL J., "The Heart." *Scientific American,* May, 1957, p. 74.

CHAPTER 3

Nutrition

INTRODUCTION

Animals, like all living things, constantly expend energy in their metabolism. Plants are able to utilize the visible wave lengths of light in the process of photosynthesis by which carbohydrates are manufactured from CO_2 and water. In this process light energy is converted to chemical energy which is stored in the carbohydrate molecules. When needed later, this energy may be released by the oxidation of the carbohydrates. The synthetic abilities of plants are not limited to photosynthesis. They obtain other organic compounds from chemical transformation of carbohydrates. Nitrates and sulfates, for example, are used in making amino acids, and from the amino acids, the plants produce proteins, vitamins and thousands of other organic compounds.

Unlike plants, animals are unable to utilize sunlight as an energy source. Energy must be supplied in the constituents of their food. For this reason, animals are dependent upon plants, either directly or indirectly, for their nutrients. This is apparent for herbivorous animals, since they consume plants directly. Carnivorous animals, which eat either herbivores or other carnivores, are still ultimately dependent on plants. This is why we say plants are the primary producers of food chains.

Consider a food chain which might be represented by the following series of plants and animals in a pond community:

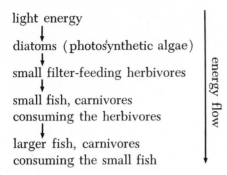

It is conceivable that this community would persist for some time because all the animals have a food supply. What would happen, however, to the fish if the herbivores were not there? And what would happen to both of them if the algae disappeared? It is obvious that if one group of plants or animals is not present, the remainder of the food chain cannot exist.

As indicated above, the resulting food chain involves a transfer of energy from one feeding, or trophic, level to the next. The total energy of the system is constant, that is, the energy entering the confined community equals the energy leaving. However, these transformations are never 100% efficient; some energy is always lost in unusable forms such as heat, so that the plants transfer more chemical energy to the herbivores than the herbivores give to the carnivores in the series. This lack of complete energy transfer follows the second law of thermodynamics which will be discussed in Chapter 6.

The major nutrients for animals, as noted above, are derived directly from plant tissues, or secondarily from the tissues of other animals. From these nutrients additional constituents are synthesized either by the animal's own tissues or by the microbial inhabitants (plants and animals) of the intestinal tract.

An enormous array of food-gathering mechanisms has evolved among animals. Sessile or slow-moving aquatic animals such as clams, sea anemones, barnacles, and many tube-dwelling worms gather food by filtering the water. Other animals such as spiders, caddis flies and ant lions build webs and nets and pitfalls. In other groups, mechanisms of predation or escape have evolved such as teeth, talons, poisons, flight, sensitive sight, hearing and smell.

MECHANISMS OF DIGESTION

The gathering and ingesting of quantities of food is not all that is required for successful nutrition. The food must be of the right quality and must be degradable. Most food is made up of large organic compounds which are weakly ionized and rather unreactive. In addition, the tissues of animals exist at relatively low temperatures, say between 10°C and 40°C, which further limits reaction rates. All chemical reactions, including those of biological importance, proceed toward an equilibrium. However, the rate at which they proceed may be extremely slow. *Enzymes* are special proteins which catalyze these slow biological reactions and hasten the achievement of equilibrium. They do not, however, alter the point where equilibrium is reached. Enzymes are generally specific for a particular reaction. They contain an active site, a relatively small part of the molecule, which is capable of combining reversibly with a specific substrate. The enzyme is not used up in the reaction it catalyzes, it simply performs its special operation on one substrate molecule after another. Another common characteristic of enzymes is the requirement for certain cofactors. The cofactor may be a vitamin, a small organic compound or a trace metal. Without such cofactors, many enzymes are almost completely inactive.

The activity of an enzyme depends upon its molecular shape and the ionized groups it possesses. Factors determining shape and ionization of proteins include pH, temperature and the metals or salts of the fluids surrounding them. It is not surprising, therefore, that the digestive enzymes must operate in an appropriate hydrogen ion and salt medium within the gastrointestinal tract. In addition, enzymes are labile at temperatures above 50°C to 70°C, as are other proteins. The change in shape and ionization of proteins which results from exposure to acids, alkali, heavy metals or high temperatures is called denaturation. If the active portion of an enzyme becomes denatured, it of course cannot function as a catalyst.

Digestive enzymes catalyze mainly hydrolyses, that is, cleavage reactions which incorporate water into the products. Ingested carbohydrates include the polysaccharides starch and glycogen, the disaccharides such as sucrose and lactose, and the simple sugars or monosaccharides such as glucose and fructose. Polysaccharides and disaccharides require hydrolysis to simple sugars before they can be absorbed across the intestinal wall. Similarly, the fats in food are usually in the form of triglycerides. Although much of the fat is absorbed directly as the triglyceride, hydrolytic enzymes, the lipases[1], reduce some of the fat to glycerol and fatty acids prior to absorption. Proteins are degraded to their amino acid con-

---

[1]The suffix *-ase* denotes an enzyme, for example *sucrase* and *lactase* are sugar-splitting enzymes, lipase is active in the conversion of fats (lipids) to fatty acids and glycerol, and protease is a generic name for protein-splitting enzymes.

stituents in preparation for absorption. Utilization of food therefore requires the synthesis and release of the appropriate enzymes and the provision for an adequate medium in which the enzymes can operate.

Initial grinding of food is common in most animals. The efficiency of enzymatic degradation depends to a considerable extent upon this process. The most powerful proteases, for example, can make little headway on the proteins of a large cube of uncooked muscle, but if it is mascerated to increase its surface area and to render it partially soluble, enzymatic degradation may proceed at a rapid pace. The teeth of mammals, the gizzards of birds and the stomach ossicles of the crustaceans exemplify some of the common structures that have evolved for this purpose. The mixing of the food mass with the enzymes is equally important in promoting digestion and absorption. This is accomplished by peristaltic movements and by the grinding or churning motions provided by the muscles of the gastrointestinal tract.

One of the largest carbohydrate deposits in nature is the cellulose of plants. Relatively few animals have the appropriate enzymes to make the initial breakdown of cellulose to the glucose of which it is composed. Several of the mammalian herbivores have evolved a "fermentation tank" in their stomachs (ruminants such as cattle or sheep), or in their lower intestines (the caecum of horses and rabbits) which maintain bacterial and protozoan cultures that degrade cellulose. Similarly, termites and wood-eating cockroachs, maintain cultures of protozoa in their intestines which accomplish the same feat. In other herbivores or omnivores, ingested cellulose remains largely unutilized. This does not mean that other animals do not harbor an intestinal microbial population. In fact, microbes are present in large numbers in all intestinal tracts, and contribute to the host's nutrition by the synthesis of vitamins and certain amino acids.

SITES OF DIGESTION

Digestion may proceed either intracellularly or extracellularly. Most of the protozoans, sponges and flatworms engulf or ingest relatively small food particles, digest them within the cells, then egest the remains. In the coelenterates, annelids, molluscs, arthropods and echinoderms, digestion is largely extracellular, although some intracellular digestion does occur in the special glands or pouches off the main gut. Among the vertebrates, digestion may be considered as essentially extracellular.

ABSORPTIVE PROCESSES

Absorption of sugars, fats and amino acids occurs across the inner-most lining or epithelium of the small intestine or some comparable segment of the gut. The same factors which determine transport across cell membranes and capillaries are operative in intestinal absorption. The numerous diverticula of the digestive glands of crustaceans, molluscs, insects and echinoderms provide large surface areas through which digestive enzymes are released and through which absorption can occur. In the vertebrates, intestinal surface area is increased enormously by the presence of finger-like villi. Generally, a large capillary bed in the intestinal wall provides a means of transporting the absorbed materials to the liver or to some comparable structure.

Simple diffusion plays some role in absorption from the intestine, but active transport (see Chapter 2) is also required, particularly for the sugars and amino acids. Fat absorption is often enhanced by the detergent action of bile salts released from the gall bladder. These salts emulsify the fat, rendering it more accessible to lipases and to direct absorption. At least part of the emulsified fat is absorbed directly as the neutral triglyceride and is carried into the circulation by the lymphatic vessels of the intestine.

UTILIZATION OF NUTRIENTS

Briefly, the fates of the major nutrients within an animal may be summarized as follows:

1. Carbohydrates — Oxidized as fuel; utilized in such structural components as cell membranes, tendons, chitin etc.; stored to a limited extent as glycogen.
2. Fats — A major fuel source; serve as structural components of membranes, mitochondria and other organelles of the cells; serve as an energy store.
3. Protein — Used to a limited extent as fuel. Ingested protein is degraded to its constituent amino acids which in turn are synthesized into the proteins characteristic of the consumer's tissues, including structural proteins, contractile proteins of muscle, enzymes etc.
4. Vitamins — Function as coenzymes for the respiratory enzymes (B vitamins) or as components in specific reactions such as Vitamin A in vision, Vitamin D in calcium metabolism and Vitamin K in blood clotting.
5. Minerals — The major minerals such as Na^+, K^+ and Cl^- constitute the salts of the body fluids. Iron is incorporated into the heme of

hemoglobin, myoglobin and the respiratory enzymes such as the cytochromes. Copper is part of some cytochromes, while cobalt is part of vitamin B_{12}. In addition, zinc, molybdenum, manganese, magnesium and calcium are required for activity of specific enzymes. Phosphate and calcium are used in the skeletons of many animals. Perhaps even more importantly, phosphates form the ester bonds which store most of the chemical energy of animal and plant tissues in such compounds as adenosine triphosphate (ATP) and creatine phosphate (CP). Iodine is required as part of the thyroid hormone molecule.

DIETARY REQUIREMENTS

The major fuel compounds, the carbohydrates and fats, are supplied largely by the diet. The amino acids and vitamins are derived from dietary sources, from the synthetic activities of the intestinal flora and from syntheses in the tissues. Only some of the amino acids, fatty acids and vitamins must be ingested directly. Those amino acids which must be supplied in the diet in order to maintain growth and nitrogen balance are called the *essential amino acids.* In man these include, arginine, histidine, isoleucine, leucine, lysine, methionine, phenylalanine, threonine, tryptophan and valine. There remain approximately ten additional amino acids that are obtained by synthesis within the tissues as long as adequate amounts of the essential amino acids are provided.

Lipid requirements are less specific than those for amino acids. There is, however, a requirement for unsaturated fats[2] in the diet of some mammals (e.g., the rat and probably man), but not for others (such as the mouse and the dog). Approximately one-third of the total calories[3] of man's diet are derived from the oxidation of fat. If more than half the diet is composed of lipids, there is typically a deposition of fat which may lead to obesity. The carbohydrate requirements, like those for lipids, are not specific, but the supply must be adequate to provide from one-half to two-thirds of the total calories.

----

[2]Stearic and linolenic acids are examples of saturated and unsaturated fatty acids respectively.

$CH_3(CH_2)_{16}COOH$ stearic acid (no double bonds; i.e., a fat "saturated" with hydrogen.)

$CH_3CH_2CH=CHCH_2CH=CHCH_2CH=CH(CH_2)_7COOH$ linolenic acid (with double bonds, an unsaturated fat.)

[3]Calorie — a measure of heat (energy); the heat required to raise the temperature of 1 gram of water from 14.5 to 15.5°C. 1000 calories = 1 kilocalorie.

The vitamins which are essential in the diet of man include thiamine, niacin, riboflavin, folic acid, pyridoxine, vitamin B_{12}, and vitamins A, C, D, E, and K. Several of these are synthesized by intestinal microorganisms, e.g., vitamin K, thiamine, vitamin B_{12} and riboflavin, but in inadequate amounts for maintaining the host. The remaining vitamins, biotin, pantothenic acid, inositol, lipoic acid, and choline are said to be nonessential since they are obtained in adequate amounts from the general diet, from the microbes and from tissue synthesis.

Prolonged inadequacies of certain vitamins lead to characteristic deficiency diseases such as scurvy (inadequate vitamin C), rickets (vitamin D) and beriberi (thiamine). It is difficult to produce deficiencies of other vitamins such as riboflavin or pantothenic acid, since they are obtained in part from the synthetic activities of the intestinal microorganisms. Niacin, too, is obtained in part from intestinal microbial synthesis and from synthesis in the liver. As a result, niacin deficiency (pellagra) apparently appears only when there is an inadequate dietary source of both the vitamin and its precursor amino acid, tryptophan. Although biotin is supplied largely by the microbes of the intestine, a deficiency may be produced by the novel means of ingesting uncooked egg white. The albumen of eggs include the protein avidin, which binds biotin in an inactive complex. The lipid-soluble vitamins (A, D, E and K) are stored in considerable quantities in the fatty tissues of the body so that prolonged deprivation is required for any deficiency symptoms to appear. There is no corresponding storage of the water-soluble vitamins. Finally, it should be noted that in large doses, almost any vitamin can be toxic, particularly the fat-soluble ones which tend to accumulate.

COMPARISON OF DIGESTION IN A RUMINANT AND AN OMNIVORE

Digestion and absorption processes differ widely among animals, even within the mammals. Fig. 3-1 summarizes the contrasting conditions in the digestive processes of omnivores such as man or swine with those of ruminants such a cattle or sheep. In man, the stomach is relatively small. The secretion of hydrochloric acid and the protease, pepsin, initiates protein digestion. Bile salts from the liver enhance fat emulsification. The pancreatic secretions include considerable amounts of sodium bicarbonate which neutralizes the acid from the stomach, thus preparing the fluid medium for the enzymes of the pancreas and small intestine which operate in a slightly alkaline medium (Fig. 3-1A). Most of the absorption of nutrients occurs in the small intestine, although significant amounts of salt and water are absorbed from the large intestine.

A. Omnivore Digestion

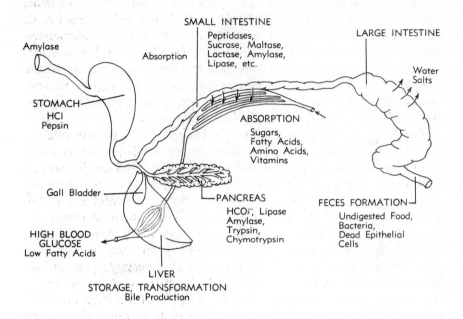

Amylase

STOMACH
HCl
Pepsin

Gall Bladder

HIGH BLOOD
GLUCOSE
Low Fatty Acids

LIVER
STORAGE, TRANSFORMATION
Bile Production

Absorption

SMALL INTESTINE
Peptidases,
Sucrase, Maltase,
Lactase, Amylase,
Lipase, etc.

ABSORPTION
Sugars,
Fatty Acids,
Amino Acids,
Vitamins

PANCREAS
HCO₃⁻, Lipase
Amylase,
Trypsin,
Chymotrypsin

LARGE INTESTINE

Water
Salts

FECES FORMATION
Undigested Food,
Bacteria,
Dead Epithelial
Cells

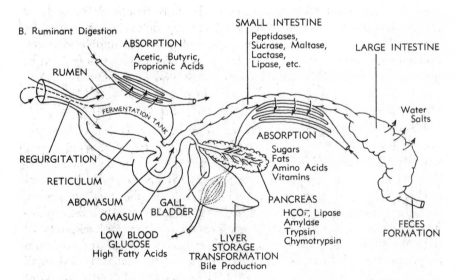

B. Ruminant Digestion

RUMEN

ABSORPTION
Acetic, Butyric,
Proprionic Acids

FERMENTATION TANK

REGURGITATION

RETICULUM

ABOMASUM

OMASUM

GALL
BLADDER

LOW BLOOD
GLUCOSE
High Fatty Acids

LIVER
STORAGE
TRANSFORMATION
Bile Production

SMALL INTESTINE
Peptidases,
Sucrase, Maltase,
Lactase,
Lipase, etc.

ABSORPTION
Sugars
Fats
Amino Acids
Vitamins

PANCREAS
HCO₃⁻, Lipase
Amylase
Trypsin
Chymotrypsin

LARGE INTESTINE

Water
Salts

FECES
FORMATION

Fig. 3-1. Diagram comparing the digestive and absorptive processes of (A) an omnivore such as man, with (B) ruminants such as cattle, sheep or deer.

Ruminant digestion and nutrition (Fig. 3-1B) differs markedly from that just described for a typical omnivore. The ruminant stomach is divided into four subcompartments, the rumen, reticulum, omasum and abomasum. It is large, having a capacity of 40 or more gallons in a large cow. The rumen and reticulum contain the microbes which digest cellulose. These bacteria and protozoa operate in an almost neutral environment in contrast to the acid fluids of the stomachs of omnivores and carnivores. This huge fermentation tank allows the ruminant to consume extremely rough fodder and obtain almost all the required nutrients from it. The bacteria and protozoa produce large quantities of acetic, proprionic and butyric acid from the degraded cellulose. The host absorbs some of these substances directly from the stomach (Fig. 3-1B). In the cow, as much as 90% of the caloric requirement is obtained from these compounds. In general, ruminants have low circulating blood glucose levels (50 mg per 100 ml blood, as compared to 100 mg per 100 ml blood in man) but have relatively large amounts of plasma fatty acids. The fatty acids are converted to fat or carbohydrate as needed. The microbial culture also synthesizes virtually all the required amino acids and vitamins from the fatty acids as long as a nitrogen source such as ammonium salts or urea is supplied. In fact, urea is converted to protein by the ruminant so effectively that commercial dairy feeds are often enriched with it. In addition, considerable evidence indicates that, on a low protein diet, some ruminants are able to absorb urea from the blood into the rumen where it is reutilized in synthesizing protein. Ruminants must of course share the food with their microbial symbionts. They must also manage to get rid of the gas produced in the fermentation, including such compounds as methane and carbon dioxide. Some of the microorganisms themselves are killed and digested as the food mass passes into the abomasum, which is the acid-producing portion of the ruminant stomach. In the small intestine, the conventional digestive and absorptive processes continue as in other mammals.

REFERENCES

PROSSER, C. L., and BROWN, F. A., JR., *Comparative Animal Physiology*, 2nd ed. Philadelphia: W. B. Saunders Co., 1961. Ch. 4, 5.

RAMSAY, J. A., *A Physiological Approach to the Lower Animals*, Cambridge University Press, 1952. Ch. 1.

RODGERS, T. A., "The Metabolism of Ruminants." *Scientific American*, February, 1953, p. 34.

SCHEER, BARDLEY T., *Animal Physiology*, New York: John Wiley and Sons, Inc., 1963. Ch. 9.

WHITE, A., HANDLER, P., and SMITH, E. L., *Principles of Biochemistry*, 3rd ed. New York: McGraw-Hill Book Co., 1964.

CHAPTER 4

Excretion and osmoregulation

INTRODUCTION

Cells continually release byproducts of their metabolism which enter the extracellular fluids. These substances leave the cells, either by diffusion or active transport, and eventually enter the circulation. Occasionally, because of incidental intake or due to action of osmotic forces, excessive amounts of salts or water may also accumulate. These substances must be either stored, tolerated or eliminated. Since there is little storage, and often only a narrow tolerance, virtually every animal, regardless of its structural simplicity, possesses some organ or organelle which performs the functions of excretion and osmotic regulation. Our purpose here will be to examine the structure and function of a few of the representative excretory systems.

KIDNEY

Vertebrate kidneys are composed of functional units called *nephrons* (Fig. 4-1) which vary in number from several thousand in amphibians to two million in mammals. There is considerable variation in the morphology of various vertebrate nephrons, particularly in regard to their length and the presence or absence of the middle segment, the loop of Henle. True Henle's loops are characteristic only of the nephrons of birds and mammals, although structurally similar segments are present in the nephrons of some of the lower vertebrates. In addition, the glomeruli of freshwater fish and amphibians are generally larger than those of

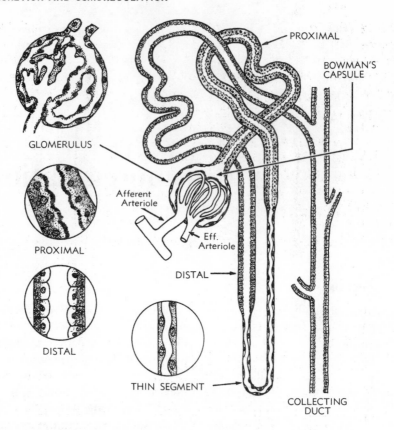

PROXIMAL

BOWMAN'S CAPSULE

GLOMERULUS

Afferent Arteriole

PROXIMAL

Eff. Arteriole

DISTAL

DISTAL

THIN SEGMENT

COLLECTING DUCT

Fig. 4-1. Diagram of a mammalian nephron, its blood supply and associated collecting duct. (From H. W. Smith, **The Physiology of the Kidney,** Oxford Univ. Press, New York, 1937.)

reptiles, birds or mammals. In certain marine fish, however, the glomeruli have undergone a remarkable regressive evolution to the point that they are virtually non-existent, at least in the adults. Each of these variations has a functional significance which will be touched upon in a later discussion.

There are essentially three related activities involved in urine formation in kidneys. 1. A filtration of plasma across the glomerular blood vessels into Bowman's capsule. 2. Both active and passive (osmotic) reabsorption of water and dissolved substances from the tubules back into the plasma. 3. A passive diffusion and an active transport (secretion) of substances from the interstitial space and the circulation (peritubular capillaries) into the tubular fluid. Some mammalian and avian kidneys are able to achieve a concentration of solutes in the urine which is higher than the plasma concentration. This involves an additional process, "a countercurrent exchange" which operates in conjunction with active transport and diffusion.

GLOMERULAR FILTRATION

The filtration process which takes place in Bowman's capsule is essentially the same as that already described in Chapter 2 in the discussion of capillary filtration. The resulting ultrafiltrate therefore contains most of the constituents of plasma except the larger proteins.

Since the proteins do not leave the circulation very rapidly, they exert a constant osmotic pressure which opposes filtration. Also, some pressure is dissipated in forcing the fluid through the membranes and in displacing fluid on the other side. As a result of these factors, the effective filtration pressure is only about 20 mm Hg. The pressures contributing to the filtration process may be summarized as follows:

[Blood Pressure (65 mm Hg)] − [Protein Osmotic Pressure (25 mm Hg) + Resistance of the Membranes (10 mm Hg) + Pressure in Bowman's Capsule (10 mm Hg)] = [Effective Filtration Pressure (20 mm Hg)]. $\hspace{2cm}$ (9)

It should be noted that some substances are bound to the blood cells and the plasma proteins. When such binding occurs, the compound in question will fail to appear in the filtrate.

What is the rate of filtration? In order to find this, we must first become familiar with the concept of *clearance*. Clearance (C) is the quantity of plasma cleared of a substance per unit time (units, ml/min.). For example, suppose the plasma contains 5 mg/100 ml of substance (x). Furthermore, assume that an analysis shows 5 mg/min. of (x) appearing in the urine. The clearance of (x) is therefore 100 ml/min. Many substances readily diffuse across the tubule walls, either entering the filtrate or leaving it. A few substances, such as the polysaccharide inulin or the endogenous compound creatinine, however, enter the tubular fluid only with the filtrate from Bowman's capsule and do not diffuse out or in. The clearance of such substances tells us the glomerular filtration rate since their rate of excretion is determined only by the filtration process. The following relationship is used for calculating glomerular filtration rate (GFR).

$$\text{GFR} = \frac{(U_{conc.}) \times (V_{flow})}{(P_{conc.})} = C_{in} \hspace{1cm} (10)$$

$U_{conc.}$ = urine concentration of inulin; V_{flow} = urine flow in ml/min.: $P_{conc.}$ = plasma concentration of inulin and C_{in} = clearance of inulin. The glomerular filtration rate, or clearance of inulin is obtained in units of ml/min. In actual practice inulin is infused intravenously at a slow rate to maintain a relatively constant plasma concentration. The urine flow and the urine and plasma concentrations of inulin are then recorded for calculations involving equation (10).

The GFR in man is about 125 ml/min. This filtrate is greatly reduced in volume and altered in composition before it is voided as urine. The actual urine formation rate is about 1-2 ml/min. The rate of fluid reabsorption from the filtrate in the tubules is thus about 123-124 ml/min. The kidney therefore normally reabsorbs more than 99% of the fluid that is filtered.

Only a fraction of the plasma flowing through the kidney appears as filtrate (Filtration Fraction). Renal plasma flow (RPF) in man is about 650 ml/min. From our value of glomerular filtration rate (GFR) we obtain:

$$GFR/RPF = 125/650 = 19.2\% = \text{Filtration Fraction}$$

To reiterate, the kidneys filter only about 1/5 of the plasma which flows through them. The filtration fraction may be modified to some degree by changes in the diameters of the efferent and afferent arterioles supplying the glomeruli (Fig. 4-1). Constriction of the efferent arterioles tends to raise blood pressure and thus increase the filtration while constriction of the afferent arterioles effectively diminishes filtration.

Much of the fluid and solute reabsorption which occurs in the proximal tubules is directed by osmotic forces. This reabsorption is said to be passive, and is analogous to that occurring from the interstitial fluids into the systemic capillaries. As the filtrate is formed, protein remains behind and exerts an osmotic force which draws fluids out of the kidney tubules into the surrounding capillaries. This occurs when the pressure in the blood vessels drops below 25 mm Hg and the net force of the protein osmotic pressure becomes effective. In addition, ions and organic substances are reabsorbed actively from the proximal tubule, a process which osmotically carries still more fluid out of the tubules. The final adjustments in solute and water to form the urine occur in the loop of Henle, the distal tubules and the collecting ducts by diffusion, active absorption and secretion.

A useful index to the handling of compounds by the kidney may be obtained from the measurement of "clearance ratio," defined as the ratio of the clearance of some substance (x) to the clearance of inulin

($C_x/C_{in.}$). Inulin only enters the urine by filtration, and once in the tubular fluid, it remains there. If a compound shows a higher clearance than inulin, it may be assumed to be secreted into the tubules; if a lower clearance, it is reabsorbed by either active transport or by diffusion. The clearance of urea in man is less than that of inulin, being about 60 ml/min., which gives a clearance ratio ($C_{urea}/C_{in.}$) of approximately 0.48. This indicates that urea is readily filtered but not actively secreted into the tubular fluid and that some of the filtered molecules are reabsorbed.

The urine to plasma concentration ratio (U/P) of a substance may be useful in a similar way, since it indicates the magnitude by which the kidney alters the filtrate. For example, a substance which is effectively filtered, but is not reabsorbed readily by diffusion or active transport might appear in fairly high concentrations in the urine (high U/P ratio) if there is appreciable water reabsorption. The U_{urea}/P_{urea} ratio in man may exceed 60 or 70, which reflects the water reabsorption from the tubular fluid and indicates that back diffusion of urea out of the tubule is not sufficient to establish equilibrium with plasma. It also demonstrates that the compound can be concentrated to a sufficient extent in the urine to realize an effective excretion from the body even without active transport.

Many substances present in the plasma and in the initial filtrate do not normally appear in the urine. For example, glucose, amino acids, vitamins and many other vital organic compounds are actively transported out of the filtrate as it flows through the proximal tubules. As noted in the previous chapters, active transport is an energy-requiring process, since in the final stages the movement of molecules takes place against an appreciable concentration gradient. Active transport in the nephron is largely confined to the proximal and distal portions of the tubules where the cells are beautifully constructed for efficient secretory activity. These cells are generally cuboidal in shape with a dense supply of mitochondria. In addition, the proximal tubules are lined internally with brush borders which greatly increase their surface area. The cells of the loop of Henle apparently do not contribute greatly to the active transport processes but are instead involved in the countercurrent concentrating function of nephrons (see later discussion).

Active transport in an intact kidney is exemplified by the handling of glucose. At normal plasma levels, the typical kidney reabsorbs all but the last traces of the filtered glucose. If one assumes a value of 1 mg/ml as the normal plasma glucose level, and if one uses our previous figure of 125 ml/min for the glomerular filtration rate, the rate of glucose reabsorption is 125 mg/min. If the plasma glucose level is artificially or pathologically elevated to about 2 mg/ml, however, sugar begins to appear in the urine. At this point, almost 250 mg/min are being reabsorbed. If the level is elevated to 3 mg/ml the kidney reabsorbs only about 300 mg/min and 75 mg/min. appears in the urine. Finally, at plasma levels of 5 mg/ml the amount reabsorbed remains near 300 mg/min while 325 mg/min are lost. Active transport is assumed to involve specific sites on the cell membrane. At these sites the transported substances are thought to be combined with carrier molecules (see Ch. 2). In related reactions, energy is supplied to transport them across the cell membrane. In the case of glucose, the direction of movement, a property of the transporting machinery, is from the filtrate toward the surrounding capillaries. At the concentration where the active reabsorption rate levels off, we believe that all the available transport sites are saturated with glucose, and that reabsorption has become limited by the number of sites and perhaps also by the available energy. The active site concept also includes the notion of specificity. Compounds of similar molecular structure may therefore compete for the same active transport sites in the kidney.

Active transport of some substances occurs in the opposite direction, that is, from the plasma into the tubules. R. Forster at Dartmouth showed that if one carefully dissects the kidneys from a fish or frog and places them into a compatible saline solution, they will remain active for many hours. The organs may then be teased into small parts to give isolated pieces of tubules. If some of the fragments are placed in a saline containing phenol red, one can observe, after 15 minutes or so, a concentration of dye within the tubule. The dye is transported actively, as

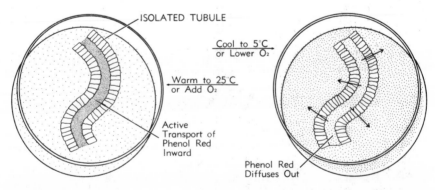

Fig. 4-2. Forster's method for observing active transport in isolated kidney tubules.

evidenced by the higher concentration in the lumen of the tubule (Fig. 4-2). If one removes the oxygen supply, lowers the temperature, or adds a metabolic poison, the active process is deprived of its energy supply and the accumulated dye diffuses out. The kidney tubules of certain marine fish, i.e., the flounder, are "aglomerular." Such kidneys offer particularly useful material for studying active transport by the dye method, because the normal mechanism of urine formation is secretion (active transport) rather than filtration. The aglomerular kidney probably has evolved in some marine fishes as one mechanism for conserving water. Since the usual filtration process does not occur, the requirements for massive fluid reabsorption are eliminated.

THE CONCENTRATING KIDNEY

The desert environment presents a host of problems for survival, including the legendary scarcity of water and the extremes in temperature. These difficulties are compounded because water and temperature regulation are so intimately linked. For example, when the environmental temperature exceeds the body temperature, the animal gains heat by radiation and conduction from the surroundings, and the only avenue for heat loss which remains is the evaporation of water. If water is not used under these conditions, the body temperature may rise to lethal levels. On the other hand, if too much water is used, the body fluids become depleted, which is equally lethal. In spite of these harsh realities, the deserts support a wide variety of plant and animal life. When adequate water is available, most animals, including man, can survive in a relatively hot desert, but when water becomes limited, as it is for most desert species, some special adaptations are necessary to prevent dehydration. One of the most basic adaptations which has evolved for conserving water involves the concentrating kidney; that is, a kidney which is able to produce a urine considerably more concentrated than the plasma.

A number of desert rodents, such as the kangaroo rat, the gerbil, and the sand rat have particularly well-developed concentrating kidneys. Kangaroo rats are capable of producing urine containing 7% salt and more than 20% urea. This results in a urine-to-plasma osmotic pressure ratio of about 14 to 1. If forced to drink sea water (3.5% salt), man becomes dehydrated since his urine at best contains only about 2% salt. For every liter of sea water consumed, man must therefore produce 1.75 liters of urine to remove the salt. K. and B. Schmidt-Nielsen at Duke University showed that a kangaroo rat, on the other hand, can survive well while drinking sea water by eliminating the salts in a much more concentrated urine. In fact when fed only dry seeds kangaroo rats can survive almost indefinitely without drinking water.

How is this accomplished? Do the renal cells actually pump ions against a concentration gradient of 14 to 1? It turns out that they need not work against such a large gradient in order to produce urine which is 14 times as concentrated as the plasma. By means of a counter-current multiplier system, a concentrated urine is produced, but the individual cells move ions against a relatively low gradient. Reference to Fig. 4-3 will illustrate the essentials of the mechanism. The ability to produce a highly concentrated urine depends in part on the morphology of the nephrons. Very long loop nephrons increase the ability to maintain a large longitudinal gradient with a relatively low horizontal gradient (Fig. 4-3). In various mammals and birds, there is a good correlation between the presence of long loop nephrons and the ultimate concentrating ability of the kidney. It should be noted also, that the tubules form "hairpin loops" that allow the fluid to move in opposite directions yet in close proximity in the two arms of each loop. In addition, the tubules are small and tightly packed, which further enhances the transfer of materials from one to another. The initial development of the large longitudinal gradient requires the active transport of sodium out of the ascending limb of the loop of Henle. As the Na^+ is pumped out of the ascending limb, it enters the interstitial fluid and diffuses into the descending limb. Note again that the horizontal gradient against which the sodium pump is operating is relatively small. The flow carries the Na^+ into the medullary portion of the kidney. The formation of a concentrated urine depends largely upon the osmotic withdrawal of water from the fluid in the collecting ducts.

How is the concentrating kidney able to produce anything other than a hyperosmotic urine? This is done apparently by two means. If the sodium pump of the ascending limb becomes inactive, the gradient will soon disappear. The control of the pump, however, is not well understood. Secondly, if the permeability of the collecting ducts is diminished, the osmotic removal of water will be correspondingly reduced. The latter control is achieved in part by the action of *antidiuretic hormone (ADH)* that is released from the neurohypophysis. This hormone is thought to act by increasing the permeability of the collecting ducts to water, thus increasing urine osmolarity. The ADH titer is controlled by receptors in the hypothalamus of the brain; a center which detects changes in the osmotic pressure of the blood. If blood osmotic pressure is low and a hyperosmotic urine is not required, the ADH titer remains low and water is retained in the collecting ducts. As blood osmotic pressure is increased,

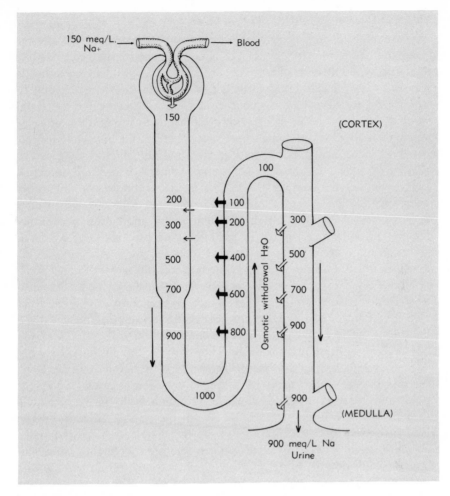

Fig. 4-3. Schematic representation of the countercurrent mechanism for concentrating urine. The heavy dark arrows indicate active transport of sodium from the ascending limb. Although capable of active transport, the ascending limb is apparently impermeable to the back diffusion of sodium once it has been extruded. The sodium does, however, enter the descending limb. Ions accumulate in the interstitial fluid and Henle loop region of the kidney (medulla). This creates a gradient that osmotically withdraws water (large open arrows) from the collecting duct producing a concentrated urine. Note that the horizontal gradient against which the pump must operate is relatively low in comparison to the resulting longitudinal gradient.

ADH is released to provide for maximal urine concentration and minimal urine volume.

OSMOREGULATION IN MARINE MAMMALS AND BIRDS

There is of course no available freshwater source for most marine mammals. Unlike the desert animals, however, they have little need of water for evaporative cooling. The water balance problem therefore is reduced to one of extracting sufficient water from the food to maintain body fluids, to excrete nitrogenous waste and to provide for the usual evaporation from the lungs. The major food sources for whales and seals consist of marine invertebrates and fish. There is an important difference in osmotic load imposed by a diet of marine fish in comparison to one of marine invertebrates. Fish contain somewhat less salt than the tissues of marine mammals, while marine invertebrates, on the other hand, are osmotically equivalent to sea water. Regardless of diet, whales and seals survive without drinking. Their major adaptation is a highly efficient concentrating kidney. In addition, they produce very dry feces and require very little water for evaporation.

Marine birds consume fish and invertebrates but lack the concentrating kidney typical of whales and seals. It has been shown by K. Schmidt-Nielsen and his colleagues at Duke that oceanic birds maintain fluid balance without drinking, by means of special salt-excreting glands — the *nasal glands*. These organs are small, comprising only about 0.1% of the body weight in most marine birds. They have a copious blood supply which is distributed to the secreting tubules in a counter-current flow. The tubules are constructed of a single layer of columnar secretory epithelium. There is a reflex control of secretion from the nasal glands involving osmoreceptors in the brain. When the osmotic pressure of the blood increases, the osmoreceptors signal the gland *via* a parasympathetic innervation. This control mechanism seems to alter the volume of secretion more than it does the salt content. It is interesting to note too, that the gland can be activated by osmotic loads of sucrose as well as salt, indicating that the receptors are not sensitive to a single ion but rather to a change in osmotic pressure. The secretion itself is composed largely of sodium chloride. Its concentration varies among species and individuals within a species, with typical values ranging from 3% to more than 5% salt. The secretion generally appears as small drops of fluid at the openings of the external nares; the bird removes the drops by shaking the head or by blowing. Several aspects of salt metabolism in a marine bird such as a sea gull are shown diagrammatically in Fig. 4-4.

Marine reptiles, such as certain sea turtles, sea snakes and the Galapagos iguanas, also possess salt glands that are capable of producing concentrated solutions of NaCl. Recently, it has been shown by J. Templeton at the University of Montana that some terrestrial lizards also have salt-secreting glands, but these differ from those of marine birds and reptiles by secreting potassium chloride rather than sodium chloride.

OTHER MECHANISMS OF OSMOREGULATION

Freshwater fishes, amphibians and crustaceans possess a higher concentration of salts in their plasma than is present in their surroundings. Since the integument is somewhat permeable, water tends

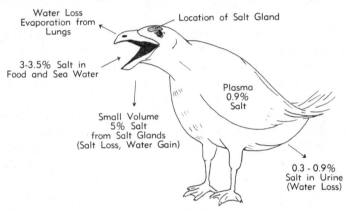

Fig. 4-4. Diagram showing some aspects of salt balance in a marine bird. The salt glands of various species are located in the nose or above the orbit.

to be drawn in osmotically, while salts "leach out." The resulting water load is partly checked by the production of a dilute and copious urine. In the freshwater fishes and crustaceans, the salt deficit is made up from the food and by active transport of NaCl from the water by special cells in the gills. Amphibians, on the other hand, are capable of actively absorbing salts through all of their skin surface (Fig. 4-5).

Marine teleosts, elasmobranchs and the relatively rare marine frogs, have the opposite problem. Sea water containing about 3-3.5% salt is more concentrated than their plasma and tends to dehydrate the animals. Marine fish drink sea water, absorb both salts and water from the intestine, but eliminate the excess salt by active secretion from the gills. They produce a sparse but dilute urine (Fig. 4-5). The elasmobranchs (sharks and rays) have evolved a different mechanism to solve the same general osmotic problem. They synthesize and retain enough urea and trimethylamine oxide in their tissues to raise their plasma osmotic pressure to equal or greater levels than that of sea water (Fig. 4-5). The marine frog

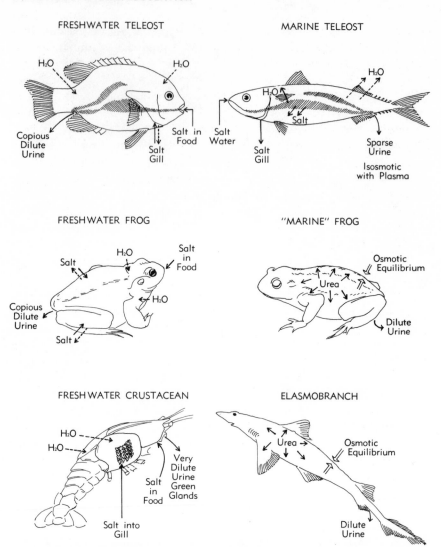

Fig. 4-5. Schematic representation contrasting the mechanisms of osmoregulation in freshwater fish, amphibians and crustaceans that face an excess of water (left) with those of marine teleosts, elasmobranchs and marine amphibians that face dehydration (right). Dashed lines represent osmotic movement; solid lines show active transport or metabolic synthesis.

referred to is the crab-eating frog of Southeast Asia, *Rana cancrivora,* which has been studied recently by M. Gordon and K. Schmidt-Nielsen. These animals live in brackish water which approaches 3% in salt concentration. By a mechanism similar to that of the elasmobranchs, they accumulate enough urea in the body fluids to equal essentially the osmotic pressure of dilute sea water. In both the sharks and the marine frogs, the salts of the plasma remain near 0.8%. The marine frog, like other amphibians, retains the active transport mechanism in the skin which takes up salts from the water, but in spite of this, it is still able to survive in a fairly concentrated saline environment (Fig. 4-5).

Osmotic and excretory functions of freshwater and marine invertebrates are similar in principle to those of the vertebrates but are considerably less complex. Virtually every animal faces some type of osmotic stress, and almost every one of them has some ability to control its internal environment. The crayfish exemplifies a rather complex freshwater invertebrate (Fig. 4-5), but lower forms also have special organs and tissues for salt transport. The contractile vacuoles of protozoa, flame cells of flatworms, nephridia of annelids and the malpighian tubules of insects are further examples of invertebrate excretory organs.

Although the body fluids of most marine invertebrates resemble sea water in total salt concentration, the individual ions are generally quite different, depending upon the permeability of the integument, and the activity of the ion-transporting tissues and excretory organs.

Some marine invertebrates have evolved these ion-regulating mechanisms to the extent that they can maintain a constant ionic make-up of their body fluids even when the environment fluctuates in composition. These animals, called *osmoregulators*, ordinarily live in river estuaries or in shallow bays where the environmental salinity may vary considerably. Other marine invertebrates, however show significant fluctuations in the salts of their body fluids when exposed to relatively small changes in salinity. The survival of such *osmoconformers* depends upon their remaining in a relatively constant marine environment.

REFERENCES

PROSSER, C. L., and BROWN, F. A., JR., *Comparative Animal Physiology*, 2nd ed. Philadelphia: W. B. Saunders Co., 1961.

SCHMIDT-NIELSEN, K., "Salt Glands." *Scientific American*, January, 1959. p. 109.

SCHMIDT-NIELSEN, K., *Desert Animals: Physiological Problems of Heat and Water*, Oxford: Clarendon Press, 1964.

SCHMIDT-NIELSEN, B., "Comparative Morphology and Physiology of Excretion," in MOORE, JOHN A., (ed.), *Ideas in Modern Biology*, Garden City, New York: Natural History Press, 1965. Ch. 14.

SMITH, H. W., *From Fish to Philosopher*, Boston: Little, Brown and Co., 1953.

SMITH, H. W., *Principles of Renal Physiology*, New York: Oxford University Press, 1956.

CHAPTER 5

Respiration and gas transport

INTRODUCTION

A primary requirement for the maintenance of living processes is the continuous expenditure of energy. In a previous chapter the ingestion, digestion and absorption of food was discussed. This section will be concerned with the processes by which energy is released from these nutrients and made available to the organism.

The energy-yielding reactions of animal tissues may be divided into aerobic and anaerobic processes. As the terms imply, the aerobic pathways require oxygen, while the anaerobic ones do not. There are a number of bacteria and a few invertebrates capable of deriving most or all of their energy anaerobically. Also, certain vertebrate tissues such as liver and skeletal muscle are able to degrade nutrients by anaerobic means. However, in most animals the aerobic pathway predominates.

The major pathways of energy release are remarkably uniform throughout the animal kingdom. Like other biological reactions, the sequence is catalyzed by a specific series of enzymes; the respiratory enzymes. Several classes of respiratory enzymes are recognized, depending upon how they function in the oxidation.

The dehydrogenases begin the sequence by catalyzing the removal of hydrogen atoms from the fuel or substrate molecule. The oxidized substrate is then acted upon by another enzyme, a decarboxylase, which splits off carbon dioxide. Hydrogen atoms, obtained from the fuel molecules, are then oxidized by the removal of electrons (e^-).

50

$$\text{Hydrogen} \xrightarrow{\text{oxidation}} e^- + \text{Hydrogen ions} + \text{energy} \qquad (11)$$

Oxygen from the environment enters the sequence by accepting the electrons. The O_2 is therefore reduced.

$$2e^- + \text{oxygen} \xrightarrow{\text{reduction}} O_2^= + \text{energy} \qquad (12)$$

A number of electron transfer enzymes, called cytochromes, catalyze this reaction. Finally, hydrogen ions react with the reduced oxygen to form water.

Briefly, this accounts for the utilization of oxygen and the appearance of CO_2 and H_2O, but what happens to the energy which is released? When fat or carbohydrate is oxidized in a flame, the reaction consumes oxygen, produces CO_2 and H_2O, and yields energy just as a biological oxidation does. The energy of direct combustion appears, however, mainly in the form of heat. Biological oxidations also produce some heat, but more importantly, a portion of the total energy is "trapped" in "high energy compounds," particularly one called adenosine triphosphate (ATP):

The energy is trapped when ATP is formed from ADP (adenosine diphosphate).

$$\text{ADP} + \text{Pi(inorganic phosphate)} + \text{energy} \longrightarrow \text{ATP} \qquad (13)$$

Once energy is incorporated into the structure of ATP it can be stored until needed. When the energy is required, it is readily available through reaction of the two terminal phosphate bonds, each of which releases about 8000 cal/mole.

$$\text{ATP} \longrightarrow \text{ADP} + \text{Pi} + 8000 \text{ cal.}$$

The direct participation of oxygen in the energy-yielding reactions leads to an oxygen demand that is proportional to the total energy requirement of the animal. Ecological and population pressures have forced organisms to occupy many diverse environments with equally different availabilities of oxygen. Energy requirements themselves vary greatly, even among closely related animals. In addition, unlike the tissue fuels, and many other tissue components, oxygen is generally not stored to any appreciable extent. As a result, a wide variety of respiratory organs, gas exchange membranes, and gas transport mechanisms have evolved. Before considering these, however, it is necessary to discuss a few of the properties of environmental oxygen.

OXYGEN OF THE ENVIRONMENT

The composition of the atmosphere near the earth's surface is essentially constant (Table 5-1), containing about 21% oxygen and nearly 78% nitrogen with only a trace of carbon dioxide. At high altitudes, the atmosphere has approximately the same percentages of the various gases, but due to the lower total pressure, the partial pressure of each component is correspondingly diminished.

TABLE 5-1

Composition of Air

Gas	Per cent	Partial pressure mm Hg
Oxygen	20. 90	158. 8
Nitrogen	78. 00	592. 8
Carbon dioxide	0. 03	0. 2
Argon, others	1. 00	7. 6

Percentages have been converted to partial pressures assuming the total atmospheric pressure to be 760 mm Hg ($\% \times 760$).

In comparison, the contents of atmospheric gases in freshwater are given in Table 5-2. Each gas dissolves independently; the final content depending upon its solubility, its partial pressure and the temperature. For example, the amount of oxygen dissolved in water at 20°C may be calculated from the Bunsen absorption coefficient, *alpha* (α), and the partial pressure of oxygen in air. *Alpha* values for the common gases are

TABLE 5-2

Atmospheric Gases Dissolved in Freshwater

Gas	ml gas/liter H_2O (20°C)	Tension
Oxygen	6. 48	158. 8
Nitrogen	8. 15	592. 8
Carbon dioxide	0. 26	0. 2

recorded in most handbooks of physics, chemistry and biology. For oxygen in water at 20°C, *alpha* = 0.03102 ml O_2/ml H_2O when equilibrated with 760 mm O_2, with the oxygen volume corrected to conditions of 0°C and 760 mm Hg. We know the air contains 20.9% oxygen. Using the following relationship to correct for local barometric conditions and multiplying by 1000 so our value will be in ml/liter, we obtain:

$$\frac{\text{bar}}{(760)} \times 0.209(1000\alpha) = \text{ml } O_2/\text{liter } H_2O \tag{14}$$

If the local barometer (bar) is 760 mm Hg. and (α) is 0.03102 we can calculate that the water contains at equilibrium:

$$(1 \times 0.209) \ (31.02) = 6.48 \text{ ml } O_2/\text{liter } H_2O$$

The amount of oxygen which will dissolve in water is strongly influenced by the temperature, generally diminishing as the temperature increases. For example, the value for *alpha* at 5°C is 0.0429 ml O_2/ml H_2O, at 10°C it becomes 0.0380 and at 25°C it is only 0.0283. Finally there is a significant reduction in the solubility of gas in salt water. The O_2 content of air-equilibrated sea water (about 3.5% salt) is approximately 20% less than the value for freshwater.

It is important to note that although the oxygen content of air is 209 ml O_2/liter of air, while water contains only 6.48 ml O_2/liter at equilibrium, the partial pressure of gas in air equals the tension of the gas in water. This means that although there is considerably less O_2 per unit volume in water, the diffusion pressure is quite sufficient for an aquatic animal to obtain adequate oxygen — as long as it does not deplete the supply.

GAS EXCHANGE SURFACES

In addition to partial pressure difference, the rate of diffusion of a gas is directly proportional to the surface area available for diffusion and to the solubility of the gas. Diffusion rate is also inversely proportional to the diffusion distance and to the square root of the molecular weight of the gas. Solubility is important even for air-breathing animals, since the gases must dissolve in the tissue fluids of the exchange membranes. Upon examining these factors, one should note that some of them are properties of the gas and the solvent (solubility and molecular weight) while others are determined by the morphology and physiology of the animals, e.g., the surface available for diffusion, the diffusion distance and the partial pressure difference. These latter three factors, being subject to evolutionary change, contribute to the diversity of respiratory surfaces and ventilation systems existing in the animal kingdom.

LUNGS

The lungs of air-breathing vertebrates are gas-exchange organs with enormous surface areas and short diffusion distances. The capillary bed of the human lung is estimated to have 50-100 square meters of surface area! The design of the lung is so efficient that equilibrium between the gases in the lung and the blood can occur in less than one second — the time an average red cell requires to pass along an alveolar capillary. This efficient diffusion process is required to meet the relatively high oxygen demand of active animals. The lungs are elastic sacs, which, along with the great arteries and veins and the heart, almost fill the thoracic cavity (Fig. 5-1). Since the cavity is sealed off except for the trachea or windpipe, the lifting of the ribs and the flattening of the diaphragm expands the thorax during breathing in or inspiration. This creates a pressure in the lung cavity which is lower than atmospheric (about 8 mm Hg less) and air is pulled into the lungs. Expiration or breathing out is largely passive. As the respiratory muscles relax, the volume of the lung cavity diminishes due to the elasticity of the lung walls. The movements of the diaphragm and rib cage which alter lung volume are controlled in part by a reflex involving stretch-sensitive nerves in the lungs and in part by the respiratory center located in the medulla of the brain. As the lungs expand fully during inspiration, the stretch receptors send signals to the respiratory center to inhibit further expansion. Passive exhalation then occurs as the chest returns to its relaxed position. Spontaneously active neurons in the respiratory center initiate the next cycle while the stretch receptors of the unexpanded lung are inactive. The rhythm of quiet breathing is therefore a result of the interaction of activity in the respiratory center and the sensory information returning from the lungs. During exercise, this basic sequence and rhythm is speeded up as the demand for oxygen increases.

The most important factor controlling the activity of the respiratory center is the level of carbon dioxide in the blood. Carbon dioxide is produced by metabolism at almost the same rate that oxygen is consumed. In addition, the gas becomes hydrated to carbonic acid. An elevated CO_2 concentration therefore signals both a higher oxygen demand and an excess of hydrogen ions (acid). The organism's response to an elevated CO_2 level is to increase the rate and depth of ventilation, a process that causes CO_2 to be expelled from the lung more rapidly and, at the same time, increases the oxygen supply.

The human lung is ventilated during rest at a rate of about 14 breaths per minute. Since each breath transports about 500 ml of air (called the tidal volume), a total of about 7 liters of air is moved into and out of the respiratory passages per minute. Only about 5 liters/minute reaches the gas exchange membranes of the alveoli, however, because it requires about 2 liters per minute to fill the dead space of the respiratory system, which includes the larynx, trachea and bronchioles. Since 5 liters of air reach the alveoli per minute, about 1 liter of oxygen is brought into

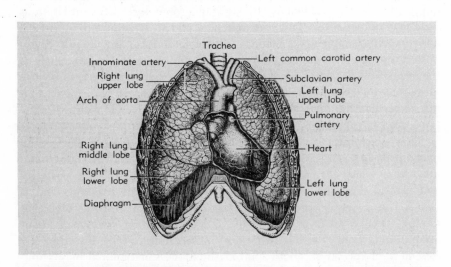

Fig. 5-1. Drawing of the organs of the human chest cavity. Essentially all of the space is filled by the lungs, heart and major blood vessels. The lungs are filled by the contraction of the diaphragm (flattening the floor of the chest cavity) and the intercostal muscles (elevation of the ribs). As the dimensions of the cavity enlarge, the pressure inside the lungs is lowered, thereby pulling air in. Exhalation (breathing out) is largely passive since relaxation of the muscles causes the chest cavity and the elastic tissues of the lungs to return to their original position. (From Tuttle, W. W. and B. A. Schottelius. **Textbook of Physiology,** 15th ed. C. V. Mosby Company, St. Louis, 1965.)

the lungs each minute (20% O_2 in air multiplied by 5 liters). An adult human at rest consumes about 200 ml $O_2/$ minute. This means that we remove about 200/1000 or 20% of the available oxygen from the air that eventually reaches the exchange membranes.

The maximum ventilation rate for man during strenuous exercise is about 100 liters per minute. This represents an increase of about 14-fold above the resting level. Cardiac output meanwhile can be expected to increase only about 5-fold, from 5 liters of blood/minute at rest to 25 liters/minute. Transport of oxygen by the blood, rather than ventilation, may therefore be the limiting process in determing maximum energy output.

GILLS

Respiratory organs which extend outward from the body surface are usually called gills. They are typical of aquatic animals such as fish, many insect larvae, crustaceans, and molluscs. Like lungs, gills generally possess thin membranes and large surfaces that are supplied with numerous capillaries or tracheoles. In addition, some form of ventilation is usually provided. Ventilation of the gills of fish is achieved by buccal and opercular movements which propel water from the mouth cavity posteriorly over the exchange surfaces. In the most active fish, such as the mackerel, it has been demonstrated that swimming is actually required to provide adequate ventilation. Movement is so critical, that mackerel may become asphyxiated in air-saturated sea water if they are forced to remain stationary!

Crayfish, lobsters and crabs utilize a pair of appendages, the second maxillipeds, as ventilation organs. These structures undergo a sculling movement which draws water into the gill chamber from the posterior and ventral directions. The water flows over the gill filaments and is expelled in a forward direction. A 10-gram crayfish at rest in water containing about 6 ml $O_2/$liter at 20°C has a ventilation volume of about 300 ml H_2O/hour. During respiratory stress, induced by lowering the oxygen of the water to about 1 ml $O_2/$liter, the same animal may pump five times as much. Bivalve molluscs, such as oysters and clams, utilize cilia to move water over the gills for both respiration and feeding. The ventilation volume of a large oyster can amount to 10-15 liters/hour.

TRACHEAL RESPIRATION

In the insects, and in most of the spiders, centipedes and millipedes, respiratory gases are carried more or less directly to and from the tissues by a vast network of fine tubes called tracheae (Fig. 5-2). The major tracheal trunks communicate with the outside of the body through special openings called spiracles. There is a repeated branching of the trunks into smaller and smaller tubules which ultimately terminate in the tracheoles. These tiny tubules (near 1 micron in diameter) are extremely numerous and actually contact or penetrate most of the cells in the body. Like the vertebrate capillary system, they provide a large and

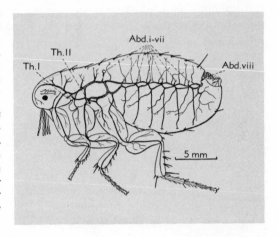

Fig. 5-2. Drawing of the left half of the tracheal system of a flea. Only the major trunks can be shown at this magnification. The spiracles, located along the abdominal (i-viii) and thoracic segments (I, II), communicate with the outside. Most of the movement of gases, at least in the smaller tracheal vessels, is accomplished by diffusion, oxygen moving toward, and carbon dioxide away from, the tissues. (From V. B. Wigglesworth, **Proc. Royal Soc., B, 118,** 1935.)

efficient system for gas diffusion. In some insects, the diameter of the spiracular opening is controlled largely by the CO_2 pressure of the tissues. They remain partially closed until the CO_2 accumulates to a certain critical level, at which time they are opened to renew the gases of the main tracheal trunks. Periodic opening and closing of the spiracles allows for adequate gas exchange and at the same time prevents excessive evaporation of water from the tracheal surfaces. If the spiracles are forced to remain open by elevated CO_2 levels, most insects in a dry environment will desiccate rapidly.

Ventilation in insects is confined mainly to movement of the gases in the larger tracheal trunks. This is generally accomplished by relatively slow and intermittent movements of the abdomen, although in some species, the thoracic movements involved in flight contribute to the process. The movement of gases along the smaller tracheae is accomplished entirely by diffusion and is directed by the concentration gradients. Such a gaseous diffusion process can supply oxygen (and remove carbon dioxide) at a very high rate without the aid of ventilation, since the diffusion distance is relatively short. The rate of diffusion of oxygen in air is about three hundred thousand times as rapid as it is in water or tissue fluids. Although the circulation and the blood is otherwise useful, it is of little importance for gas transport in tracheate animals.

An interesting problem in gas diffusion is illustrated by the plastron insects such as the 'water-boatmen' and the 'back-swimmers.' Although typically tracheate, these aquatic bugs (Order Hemiptera) are able to live under water much of the time by taking an air bubble with them when they dive. The air store is carried on a mat of non-wettable or hydrophobic hairs located in such a manner that the spiracles of the tracheal system open directly into the bubble. These animals can stay submerged much longer than the length of time accounted for by the supply of oxygen they take with them in their initial dive. This is accomplished by virtue of the gaseous diffusion across the bubble-water interface. As oxygen is consumed from the bubble, additional molecules of gas diffuse in from the surrounding water. The metabolically produced carbon dioxide enters the bubble from the spiracles and rapidly diffuses out into the water, so its concentration within the bubble remains low. Nitrogen, on the other hand, tends to accumulate, since part of the oxygen which is used is replaced by nitrogen. Eventually, therefore, either as a result of low oxygen concentration or diminishing bouyancy, the insect must surface to renew its supply. Fig. 5-3 summarizes the progressive changes which occur. When forced to dive with a bubble of pure oxygen, these insects cannot remain submerged as long as they

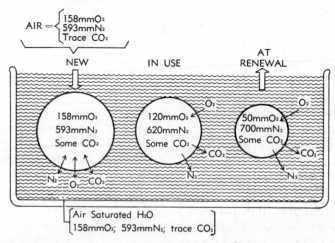

Fig. 5-3. The gas diffusion processes associated with air bubble utilization in diving insects.

can when supplied with air. Under these conditions, oxygen is not only consumed by the animal, but it also leaves the bubble by diffusion into the surrounding water where the O_2 tension is lower. Nitrogen tends to diffuse into the bubble, but due to its low solubility, it diffuses more slowly than oxygen or carbon dioxide, and as a result, the bubble quickly shrinks to a small size and the animal is forced to surface.

RESPIRATORY PIGMENTS

With the major exception of the tracheate animals, most complex forms possess a blood protein which transports oxygen and carbon dioxide. The various respiratory pigments (so-called because they are all colored proteins) include *hemoglobin, hemocyanin, hemerythrin* and *chlorocruorin.* The hemoglobins, which are the most universally distributed of the pigments, occur in some annelid worms, a few arthropods and molluscs, and in all the vertebrates. Myoglobins, the closely related muscle respiratory pigments, are found in a few invertebrates and in many vertebrates, particularly in the mammals. Hemocyanins are the major respiratory pigments of molluscs and crustaceans, while hemerythrins and chlorocruorins are confined to a few marine invertebrates. Hemoglobin is often found in cells, such as the vertebrate erythrocyte, but in some invertebrates it is dissolved in the blood. Hemocyanin and chlorocruorin are present as dissolved proteins; hemerythrin is confined to cells. All of the respiratory proteins contain a functional metal, either *iron* in hemoglobin, hemerythrin, chlorocruorin and myoglobin, or *copper* in hemocyanin.

The key functional properties of respiratory pigments are their *oxygen capacities* and their *oxygen equilibrium* characteristics. Oxygen capacity is the amount of oxygen carried when all the respiratory pigment molecules are combined with oxygen. The oxygen equilibrium curve describes how the loading and unloading of oxygen is related to the partial pressure of oxygen in the solution.

Vertebrate hemoglobins have molecular weights in the vicinity of 64,500. Each molecule is made up of four smaller protein subunits, each having a molecular weight of about 16,000. The iron of hemoglobins is bound in a nitrogen-containing organic molecule called heme. Each of the four subunits contains one heme and one iron atom. Each iron atom is capable of binding one oxygen molecule. Thus the number of hemes determines the oxygen capacity.

The globin or protein portion of hemoglobin, however, determines the affinity of the heme iron for oxygen, so that a relatively minor change in the structure of the globin influences the oxygen equilibrium. Human hemoglobin has essentially the same molecular weight, heme content and oxygen capacity as mouse hemoglobin, but the kind and sequence of amino acids in the globin portion are different, and these variations are strongly reflected in the oxygen equilibrium characteristics of the two pigments (Fig. 5-4B).

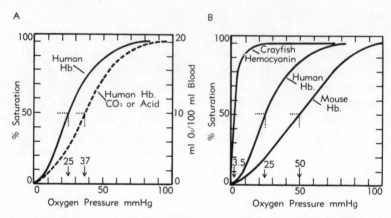

Fig. 5-4A. O_2 equilibrium curves for human Hb under normal conditions 37°C, 40 mm CO_2 and pH 7.4, and in the presence of additional CO_2 or lowered pH. The scale at the right gives the actual values of O_2 content/100 ml blood at the various O_2 pressures.

B. Comparison of O_2-affinity of crayfish hemocyanin, human hemoglobin and mouse hemoglobin. Affinity is generally given as P_{50}, the O_2 tension which yields 50% saturation.

Vertebrate bloods contain between about 10 and 15 grams of hemoglobin per 100 milliliters. When exposed (that is, equilibrated) to a gas mixture containing about 100 mm O_2, most hemoglobins become 100% saturated. When all of the hemoglobin molecules are loaded to capacity with oxygen, they are then in the form of 100% oxyhemoglobin. Human blood containing about 15 grams of hemoglobin per 100 ml of blood has an oxygen capacity of about 20 ml O_2/100 ml blood. If plasma alone is equilibrated under conditions of 100 mm O_2, it will carry only about 0.32 ml O_2/100 ml. This differential emphasizes the value of hemoglobin in transporting large amounts of oxygen.

If the oxygen level of the environment is lowered to zero, the oxyhemoglobin releases its bound oxygen and is converted to 100% hemoglobin (that is 0% saturation). The reversible binding of oxygen in relation to intermediate oxygen pressures is illustrated by the oxygen equilibrium curves shown in Fig. 5-4. Again, the hemoglobin is 100% saturated with oxygen at about 100 mm O_2 — the oxygen pressure in the lungs of mammals. In active muscle, where the oxygen pressure is extremely low, oxyhemoglobin would be expected to give up virtually all of its oxygen. At about 25 mm O_2, where the hemoglobin of human blood is half saturated (P_{50}), the curve is very steep, and the loading and unloading of oxygen is greatly effected by relatively small changes in pressure, whereas at either end of the curve a large change in pressure is necessary for the same effect.

Increased concentration of CO_2 or of hydrogen ions shifts the position of oxygen equilibrium curves to the right by lowering the affinity of hemoglobin for oxygen (Fig. 5-4A). This effect of CO_2 and of hydrogen ions on the equilibrium binding of oxygen is called the *Bohr effect*. The Bohr effect is derived from the fact that hydrogen ions are also involved in the oxygen-binding reaction. The addition of hydrogen ions to oxyhemoglobin tends to drive off oxygen.

$$H^+ + HbO_2 \rightleftharpoons HHb + O_2 \tag{15}$$

This reaction has a functional significance in the following way. As O_2-rich blood enters the tissue capillaries, the CO_2 produced by these same tissues diffuses into the blood. It is hydrated rapidly by the red cell enzyme *carbonic anhydrase* to produce hydrogen ions and bicarbonate ions.

$$CO_2 + H_2O \underset{\text{anhydrase}}{\overset{\text{carbonic}}{\rightleftharpoons}} H_2CO_3 \rightleftharpoons H^+ + HCO_3^- \tag{16}$$

The hydrogen ions can then lower the oxygen affinity and drive oxygen off the hemoglobin. Since the magnitude of the reaction is proportional to the hydrogen ion concentration, active tissues producing large amounts of CO_2 may therefore be expected to obtain additional oxygen by this means.

Hemoglobins with low oxygen affinities (see, for example mouse hemoglobin, Fig. 5-4B) are capable of unloading a considerably greater fraction of their oxygen to the tissue at any given local oxygen pressure. Comparison of the curves for mouse and human hemoglobins in Fig. 5-4 show that the mouse hemoglobin will unload more than 80% of its oxygen at a tissue oxygen pressure of 25 mm O_2, while the saturation of human hemoglobin is reduced by only 50% under these conditions. A similar difference exists between maternal and fetal hemoglobins. Fetal hemoglobin differs functionally from that of the adult in having a higher oxygen affinity. As a result, the blood of the fetus can become saturated with oxygen from the maternal circulation by diffusion of the gas from the placental tissues to the fetal circulation.

The oxygen capacity of blood with hemocyanin is considerably less than that of most bloods supplied with hemoglobin. The blood of a crayfish, for example, contains only about 3.5% hemocyanin and has an oxygen capacity of about 2.5-3.0 ml O_2/100 ml blood. This, however, represents about a 5-fold increase over the expected oxygen capacity in the absence of the hemocyanin. The most useful functional property of crayfish hemocyanin appears to be its high oxygen affinity which renders it capable of becoming loaded in environments which are extremely low in oxygen. However, it must be realized that the animal has to maintain an even lower oxygen pressure in its tissues in order to insure unloading of the oxygen.

GAS DIFFUSION IN LUNGS AND TISSUES

The movement of gases across the lung and gill membranes as well as the exchanges in the tissues is accomplished entirely by diffusion and is directed by the partial pressure gradients. Ventilation and circulation can only diminish diffusion distance and maintain maximal pressure differences for diffusion. Where diffusion is efficient and permeability is high, as in the mammalian lung, equilibration may actually be achieved. This exchange process is shown diagrammatically in Fig. 5-5. Oxygen diffusion is driven by an initial pressure difference (ΔpO_2) of about 60 millimeters between the alveolar gas and the venous blood. Within the fraction of a second required for a red cell to pass over the alveolus, the ΔpO_2 falls to 40, 20 and 10 millimeters and finally approaches equilibrium. Carbon dioxide diffusion proceeds in a similar manner, but the initial pressure difference is only about 5 millimeters. It should be noted that CO_2 is much more soluble in tissue fluids than is oxygen. Since the diffusion rate of a gas is proportional to the solubility, carbon dioxide moves rapidly across the lung membranes in spite of the low gradient.

In some respiratory surfaces, equilibrium is not always reached, but renewal of the surface layers remains just as important. Compare the theoretical gradients shown in Fig. 5-6. In (A), the pressure drop immediately across the membrane is only $P_5 - P_3$ (P = 2 units) but in (B) it is $P_8 - P_1$, or 7 units. Assuming the membranes are equal in perme-

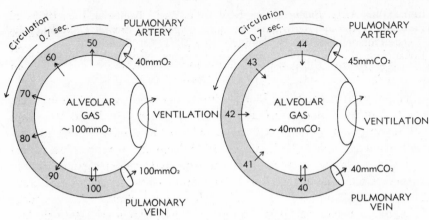

Fig. 5-5. The diffusion of O_2 from the alveoli into the pulmonary capillary blood and the corresponding movement of CO_2 into the alveoli. Diffusion approaches equilibrium in both cases.

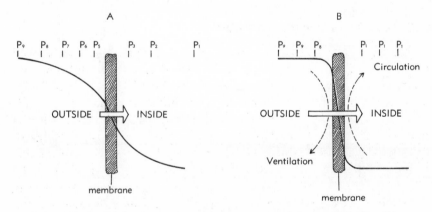

Fig. 5-6. The diffusion of a gas across an exchange membrane (A) without ventilation and circulation and (B) with renewal. Although the structure and permeability of the membranes may be the same, the gradient at the right is much steeper. P_9 . . . . . P_1 indicate diminishing pressures. The magnitude of the expected transport is roughly indicated by the relative lengths of the arrows.

ability and in thickness, the amount transferred is expected to be much greater in (B) where renewal processes are provided.

REFERENCES

KROGH, A., *The Comparative Physiology of Respiratory Mechanisms*, Philadelphia: University of Pennsylvania Press, 1941.

LEHNINGER, A. L., *Bioenergetics,* New York: W. A. Benjamin, Inc., 1965.

PROSSER, C. L., and BROWN, F. A., JR., *Comparative Animal Physiology,* 2nd ed. Philadelphia: W. B. Saunders Co., 1961. Ch. 7, 8.

ROCKSTEIN, M., (ed.), *The Physiology of Insecta,* New York: Academic Press, 1965. Vol. III, part C, Ch. 10.

CHAPTER 6

Energetics and thermoregulation

INTRODUCTION

As we have seen in the previous chapter, living organisms obtain energy by oxidation of fuel molecules. Typically, these reactions proceed through many small steps, some of which yield energy in the form of ATP. Although cells "compromise and economize" in many of their reactions, they are not able to transform energy from one form to another with 100% efficiency. In this respect, living organisms are equivalent to inanimate systems, the energy transformations of which are described by the second law of thermodynamics. There are a number of expressions which summarize this law, but for our purposes it is most easily stated as the tendency for systems to become more random. In doing so, the energy available for performing work, or the "free energy" of the system, always decreases. Consider the process of diffusion which is universal in nature. As molecules leave the area of higher concentration their arrangement becomes more random. As a result, a finite amount of energy must be applied to concentrate them again. The movement of gas molecules illustrates the same principle. As a gas expands, the system becomes more random. Energy must then be provided to compress the gas. In both of these processes, work might be accomplished if the system were appropriately harnessed, but there would always be some loss of useful energy accompanying the randomization. In summary, all systems tend toward a state of thermodynamic equilibrium where the energy available for doing work, the free energy, is minimal.

Observation shows that living cells are highly organized systems, with the component molecules being held in states far removed from equilibrium. Clearly, some form of energy is needed continually to build and maintain this complex living machinery.

An estimate of the efficiency of the energy transformations of cells can be shown by the following example. When glucose is oxidized by a cell, enough energy is obtained from each mole to synthesize 38 moles of ATP. Since each mole of ATP traps about 8000 calories, the cell derives a total of (8000 $\times$ 38) 304,000 calories from the process. When burned in a flame to CO_2 and H_2O, a mole of glucose will yield about 673,000 calories. The efficiency of the cell in obtaining energy is therefore approximately:

$$304,000/673,000 \times 100 = 45\% \qquad (17)$$

It is apparent that the chemical transformations leading to the formation of ATP alone are accompanied by a loss of more than half of the total energy. As the energy of ATP is used in the cell's synthetic activities, in active transport and for mechanical work, still more energy is lost, since all of these processes are inherently less than 100% efficient. Eventually all of the chemical energy is transformed to heat. For this reason, the rate of heat production has become the basic index of metabolic rate in living animals.

CALORIC VALUE OF FOODS: CALORIC EQUIVALENT OF OXYGEN

Carbohydrates, fats and proteins contain different amounts of carbon, hydrogen, oxygen and nitrogen (the latter in proteins only). As a result, each class of foods gives a different caloric yield. The values in Table 6-1 represent averages for common fuel sources. For example, a gram of glucose yields about 3,730 calories while a gram of starch yields about 4,400; so on the average, we estimate that carbohydrates in general give about 4,100 calories per gram.

The number of calories released expressed in terms of the volume of oxygen consumed is called the *caloric equivalent* of oxygen. This can be calculated because molecular oxygen is directly involved in the energy-yielding reactions of living organisms.

$$C_6H_{12}O_6 + 6O_2 \longrightarrow 6H_2O + 6CO_2 + 673,000 \text{ calories} \qquad (18)$$

Six moles of oxygen therefore release 673,000 calories when they are consumed in the oxidation of one mole of glucose. Since a mole of gas occupies 22.4 liters,

$$6 \text{ moles } O_2 = 6 \times 22.4 \text{ liters} = 134.4 \text{ liters } O_2 \qquad (19)$$

TABLE 6-1

Approximate Caloric Values for Common Foodstuffs

Material	calories/gram
carbohydrate	4,100
fat	9,300
protein	4,100

Taking these data, we can now calculate the caloric equivalent of oxygen for glucose as follows:

$$673,000/134.4 = \text{about } 5,000 \text{ calories/liter of oxygen} \quad (20)$$

Caloric equivalents of oxygen for other fuels, arrived at in this way, are given in Table 6-2.

We now have two possible means of arriving at the caloric output or metabolic rate of an animal. We can either measure the heat produced directly (direct calorimetry) or we may determine the rate of oxygen consumption and then calculate the rate of energy expenditure from the caloric equivalent of oxygen (indirect calorimetry). The direct measurement of the heat produced by an animal is technically difficult and requires the availability of expensive machinery. Indirect calorimetry, on the other hand, is relatively simple and has been used almost exclusively for many years.

INDIRECT CALORIMETRY AND THE MEASUREMENT OF BASAL METABOLIC RATE

In order to determine the metabolic rate by indirect calorimetry, we must know certain facts about the composition of the food source that

TABLE 6-2

Caloric Equivalents for Oxygen

Material	calories/liter O_2
carbohydrate	5,047
fat	4,686
protein	4,500

is being oxidized. This information is obtained from the respiratory quotient (R.Q.) and from the rate of nitrogen excretion.

The R.Q., which is the ratio of the volume of CO_2 produced to the volume of O_2 consumed, is obtained from a direct measurement of the gas exchange in the organism. R.Q.'s are established for each of the three classes of fuels. The R.Q. for glucose is apparent from equation 18:

$$6CO_2/6O_2 = 1 \quad \text{(the R.Q.)} \tag{21}$$

The corresponding value for fat is 0.7 and for protein 0.8. If only fat, carbohydrate or protein was being metabolized by an animal, the measurement of gas exchange would show respectively an R.Q. of 0.7, 1.0 or 0.8. If, however, one obtained an R.Q. of 0.8 for an animal on an unknown diet source, it would be incorrect to conclude that the fuel being oxidized was in fact protein, since the same value could be obtained from a mixture of fat and carbohydrate or a combination of all three fuels.

To get around this problem, one measures the nitrogen excreted in the urine and feces, as well as the oxygen uptake and carbon dioxide production. The nitrogen that is excreted comes from an equivalent amount of protein which has been metabolized. By means of a series of calculations that need not concern us here, we can work backwards from the value of nitrogen excreted and find the amount of protein from which it was derived. We can then determine by another series of calculations the amount of oxygen consumed and the carbon dioxide produced by the metabolism of this quantity of protein. If we then subtract the values for O_2 and CO_2 due to protein from the total oxygen uptake and carbon dioxide production we can arrive at a simple ratio known as the "non-protein R.Q." (N.P.R.Q.).

$$\frac{\text{(total } CO_2 \text{ produced} - CO_2 \text{ from protein)}}{\text{(total } O_2 \text{ used} - O_2 \text{ used for protein)}} = \text{N.P.R.Q.} \tag{22}$$

This procedure greatly simplifies our interpretation of the gas exchange data. The non-protein R.Q. is expected to vary from 1.0 (100% carbohydrate diet) to 0.7 (100% fat diet), depending upon the percentages of carbohydrate and fat being used. When these percentages are known, one can then calculate the number of calories produced per liter of oxygen consumed, since it will vary from 5,047 calories for 100% carbohydrate to 4,686 calories for 100% fat as fuel (see Table 6-2). These as well as some intermediate values are given in Table 6-3.

Suppose that the N.P.R.Q. was found to be 0.9 and the O_2 consumption due to non-protein metabolism was two liters during that period.

TABLE 6-3

Caloric Equivalents for O_2 at Various Non-protein R. Q. Values

Non-protein R. Q.	Per cent carbohydrate	Per cent fat	Calories/liter oxygen
1. 0	100	0	5, 047
0. 9	67	33	4, 924
0. 8	33	67	4, 801
0. 7	0	100	4, 686

Using Table 6-3, we would multiply the number of liters of oxygen times the caloric equivalent ($2 \times 4,924$) and obtain a value of 9,848 calories. We would also know from our R.Q. data that the non-protein fuel was composed of 67% carbohydrate and 33% fat (columns two and three of Table 6-3). If we add to the non-protein calories those derived from protein we can arrive at the total energy utilization of the animal during the period of observation.

This procedure works equally well for virtually all animals; the only requirement being that the energy must be released by aerobic means, that is, the fuel must be oxidized by molecular oxygen. A procedure similar to this could therefore be used whether one was working with a bird, an insect, a crab or a jellyfish. Special, rather simplified methods have been worked out for obtaining the metabolic rate of humans, since our diets are fairly uniform, our activity can be controlled, and since we have accumulated over many years a great deal of data from which certain generalizations have been drawn.

In the fasting human it has been found that a mixture of fuels are utilized which give an R.Q. of about 0.82. This R.Q. has been found to yield on the average 4,825 calories per liter of oxygen consumed. An adequate estimate of energy expenditure is therefore possible by measuring only the oxygen uptake per unit time and multiplying this value by 4,825. These assumptions and estimates are in fact routinely used when human basal metabolic rate (BMR) measurements are made.

In order to establish some standard conditions for comparison of BMR's the subject fasts for 12 hours prior to the test, and the rate of oxygen consumption is measured in the morning while the subject is at rest. A typical oxygen consumption for an adult human might be 225 ml O_2/minute. This yields a value of ($0.225 \times 4,825$) = 1,087 calories per minute. In practice the data are reduced to calories/square meter of body surface/hour. The resulting BMR can then be compared with the caloric output which is considered normal for persons of the subject's age and sex.

THE RELATIONSHIP BETWEEN BODY SIZE AND METABOLIC RATE

It has been known since early studies on animal energetics that, on a per gram basis, small animals consume more oxygen than large animals. To illustrate this, compare the following values of oxygen uptake (given here in ml/gram body weight/hour) for mammals of different size: a 20 g mouse − 1.53; a 2,500 g cat − 0.71; a 70,000 g human − 0.22; a 500,000 gram cow − 0.18. The rates of oxygen consumption for animals of intermediate body weight follow this same relationship. If one plots the logarithm of the oxygen uptake against the logarithm of the body weight, one obtains a straight line with a slope of about 0.7, as summarized by the following equation:

$$\text{Rate } O_2 \text{ consumption} = K\,(W)^{0.7} \tag{23}$$

The value K is a constant and W is the body weight. Similar equations describe the relationship between body size and metabolic rate in virtually all living organisms. In spite of its almost universal applicability, the basis of this interesting relationship is not yet understood. The suggestion has been made that the rate of oxygen consumption is related to the total body surface area. The basis of this suggestion is as follows. The surface areas of spherical objects of equal density are proportional to their weights raised to the 0.66 power. One can see that the magnitude of this exponent is very near that of equation (23). In fact, on the basis of unit surface area, the metalobic rates of animals of different size are very nearly the same. This is the fundamental reason why BMR values are presented in terms of units of body surface area rather than in terms of body weight. Unfortunately, this does not answer the basic question of why metabolic rates of small animals are greater than those of large animals on the basis of weight, but approximately equivalent on the basis of body surface area. At about the time this phenomenon was first discovered, it was pointed out that the loss of heat from animals was greater if they had a large surface and a small body weight. The question arose therefore whether the relationship derived from the fact that small animals with their large surface/weight ratios require high metabolic rates in order to maintain their body temperature. This is apparently not the explanation, since the same body size − metabolic rate relation holds for both cold blooded (poikilothermic) and warm blooded (homeothermic) animals. Another suggestion has been that perhaps the metabolic rate is correlated with the relative amount of active tissues *versus* less active tissues of the body. Although the skeleton of an elephant, for example, is relatively larger for its mass than the skeleton of a mouse, this still fails to account entirely for the observed differences in metabolic rate given in terms of body weight.

Let us ask instead how small animals obtain adequate oxygen to support their high metabolic rates. A more satisfactory answer can be given here. As we noted in the previous chapter, there are certain factors which may be modified through evolution to enhance the diffusion and transport of oxygen. The smallest animals, particularly the mammals and birds, have apparently utilized most of these. For example, lung volume is linearly related to body weight in mammals, but the alveolar area per unit of body weight is larger for the lungs of small mammals. The relative surface area available for diffusion is therefore greater in the small mammals. In addition, the concentration of capillaries is higher in the tissues of small mammals, a feature which provides an increased diffusion surface and a reduced diffusion distance. Cardiac output is generally higher per gram of tissue in the small mammals than in the large ones. This is apparently achieved by an increased heart rate in the small species, since heart size and consequently stroke volume is roughly proportional to body size. Finally, an additional adaptation involves the respiratory pigments. The hemoglobins of the smallest mammals generally have lower oxygen affinities than those of larger species. Compare, for example, the oxygen equilibrium curves for mouse and human hemoglobins shown in Fig. 5-4. The low affinity hemoglobins of small mammals unload oxygen much more readily than do the hemoglobins of the larger animals.

Assuming a small animal can obtain enough oxygen, how does it secure enough food? This is a problem for many animals, including man, and indeed, population density is often limited by the available food supply. In the smallest mammals, the time spent foraging for food occupies virtually the entire daily activity period. Apparently even this is not sufficient, as evidenced by the fact that some of the smallest mammals and birds allow their body temperatures to fall during periods of inactivity, presumably as part of a mechanism for lowering the overall metabolic demand.

TEMPERATURE AND BIOLOGICAL REACTIONS

Virtually all chemical reactions are accelerated by an increase in temperature. In order to react, a molecule must possess a critical amount of kinetic energy. In any population of molecules, some will have a great deal of energy while others will have less. As the temperature rises, more and more molecules of the population reach a sufficiently high energy level to react. As a general rule reaction rates double for each increase of ten degrees centigrade. The magnitude of this exponential increase is given by the temperature coefficient. When the coefficient is specified for a 10°C step, it is called the Q_{10}. The mathematical expression for this relationship is given by:

$$\log Q_{10} = \frac{10(\log K_2 - \log K_1)}{t_2 - t_1} \qquad (24)$$

where (K_1) is a rate function measured at temperature (t_1), and (K_2) is the same rate function measured at a higher temperature (t_2). Regardless of the temperature step, 1°C, 6°C, etc., the value of Q_{10} that is calculated from equation (24) is the factor by which the reaction rate changes with a 10°C temperature change. If the reaction rate doubles with a 10°C rise, the Q_{10} will be 2; if the rate quadruples it will be 4; and so on. For example, assume a rate (K_2) is 100 at 20°C and (K_1) is 50 at 10°C. Substituting into the equation above we obtain:

$$\log Q_{10} = \frac{10 \ (\log 100 - \log 50)}{20 - 10}$$

$$= \frac{10(2.0 - 1.699)}{10}$$

$$= 0.301 \text{ or } Q_{10} = 2$$

Since biochemical reactions also follow this general rule, one might expect the metabolic rate of a cold-blooded animal to double if the environmental temperature rises 10°C. It follows also that if a warm-blooded mammal were able to lower its body temperature, it could diminish its requirements for food, oxygen and water. As we shall discuss later in the chapter, some warm-blooded animals accomplish this by hibernating. Although one can readily measure a temperature coefficient for such functions as oxygen uptake, heart rate or ventilation rate, it should be realized that the values obtained are difficult to interpret, because they reflect the temperature coefficients of some unidentified chemical reactions underlying the processes being measured.

THE CLASSIFICATION AND EVOLUTION OF TEMPERATURE REGULATION

Most animals remain near the temperature of the surrounding air, water or soil that makes up the major substance of their environment.

Only the mammals and the birds have evolved the ability to maintain their body temperature at a constant level in spite of fluctuating environmental temperatures. We ordinarily refer to those animals which do not regulate their temperature to any great extent as "poikilotherms" or "ectotherms" because their body temperatures are controlled from the outside. Mammals and birds, on the other hand, are called "homeotherms" or "endotherms," from the fact that their temperatures are maintained by mechanisms within the body.

One might wonder why the homeothermic condition evolved only in mammals and birds. The answer is that homeothermy presents both advantages and disadvantages. The range of temperatures tolerated by active living cells is approximately 0°C to 45°C. Within this range, metabolic rates would be widely different as evidenced by our discussion of the Q_{10} rule. One can see therefore that homeothermy permits a more stable metabolic rate and renders the animal independent of a major fluctuating factor in the environment. A constant body temperature also enables animals to occupy marginal environments, where the temperature may exceed or go below the 0°C to 45°C range. Homeothermy can also insure high-speed locomotion or increased annual productivity, both of which are advantageous to the survival of the species. Homeothermy is not, however, realized without some cost to the animal. As with every other major regulatory mechanism, energy must be expended either to elevate or lower the body temperature and to maintain it.

How dependent are the poikilotherms on the dictates of the Q_{10} rule? Are their activities completely curtailed by cooling? The answer to this is definitely no, but we are not sure why. Consider the following hypothetical example. Suppose a frog is taken from its pond in the summer and tested for its ability to swim in a tank of ice water. Most likely it would have considerable difficulty and would certainly be unable to swim at the speed it does in its normal pond in the wild. If we then tested the ability of a winter frog to swim in ice water the chances are we would see a normal active performance. Is the Q_{10} rule not working? The rule is working, but the frog has undergone what we call the process of *temperature compensation*. Through a gradual acclimatization process, many poikilothermic organisms achieve an almost constant metabolic rate as the temperature changes seasonally. Although we do not yet know the mechanisms which provide for temperature compensation, one can imagine that multiple factors must be involved, including appropriate changes in biochemical pathways of synthesis and catabolism, as well as alterations in endocrine activity, circulation, excretion and active transport.

TEMPERATURE CONTROL AND THE THERMOSTAT

In maintaining constant body temperatures in the face of fluctuating environmental temperatures, homeothermic animals utilize a number of precisely controlled mechanisms for gaining and losing heat. Most of these are relatively ineffective when operating alone, but when properly coordinated they are highly efficient. The major avenues of heat gain include metabolism and the processes of conduction, convection and radiation. In contrast, heat is lost by evaporation of water and through conduction, convection and radiation. It is important to note that metabolic heat is exclusively a heat gain factor, while evaporation provides only for heat loss.

Heat transfer by radiation may result in either gain or loss, depending upon whether the animal is at a higher or lower temperature than the environment. The rate of heat transfer by this means is proportional to the fourth power of the difference in absolute temperature (absolute temperature, $T = C + 273$) between the animal and its surroundings (rate of heat transfer $\alpha \, \Delta T^4$). Conduction too, may result in a gain or loss depending upon the relative temperatures of the animal and the environment.

Convection is the transfer of heat by moving air or water. The density of the medium increases as it is cooled and diminishes as it is warmed. These local changes in density near the body surface bring about convection currents that contribute continuously to heat transfer. The rate of transfer by convection is also proportional to the velocity of the air or water movement over the body surface. The physical properties of the medium are important in determining the magnitude of heat transfer. In convection and conduction, the heat capacity and the conductivity of the medium are of major importance. Because of the higher conductivity and specific heat of water, the transfer of heat per unit of temperature difference is greater for an animal in water than for one in air.

It is possible to greatly retard the loss of heat from the body surface by insulation which may consist of a layer of air trapped in fur, feathers, or clothing, or of a layer of fat. Since trapped air is stationary, convective transfer of heat to or from the body is diminished by insulation. Similarly, the air or fat making up the insulation retards conduction generally.

Let us now consider each of these processes as they might occur in a mammal. Overall heat regulation is under the control of the hypothalamus. This center activates the required gain or loss mechanisms through the autonomic nervous system and to a lesser extent through the endocrine organs. The hypothalamus contains not only temperature receptors, but a built-in reference as well. It is in fact a thermostat. The center appears to sample the temperature of the blood as it flows through the hypothalamus. At the same time, it receives additional information from peripheral temperature receptors in the skin. The thermostat of the control center is set at 37-38°C in most mammals and near 40°C in birds. If the body temperature exceeds the reference temperature, the center instructs the autonomic nervous system to activate the heat loss mechanisms. Alternatively, if the body temperature falls below the thermostat setting, the heat gain mechanisms are activated.

During cold exposure, the blood vessels of the skin contract under autonomic control thus diminishing blood perfusion. This retards heat loss, particularly by radiation, because the skin soon cools and decreases the temperature differential between the body surface and the environment. At the same time, there may be a pilorection (fluffing of fur or feathers) which increases the thickness of the insulating air layer on the skin surface. Sweating is reduced to prevent loss of heat by evaporation. Simultaneously, metabolism is producing heat constantly. If the body temperature is sufficiently low, shivering is initiated, and this simultaneous contraction of many muscles throughout the body generates additional heat.

In the opposite case, when the body temperature rises above the hypothalamic reference, the processes described above are reversed and additional ones are activated. For example, there is generally an increased blood perfusion of the skin which brings the warm blood to the surface where heat can be readily radiated to the environment. In a hot climate where radiation, conduction and convection all lead to heat gain, the evaporation of water from the body surfaces becomes the only major avenue of heat loss. This is a very effective means under the appropriate circumstances. For example, in a dry atmosphere at 20°C about 580 calories are lost per gram of water converted to vapor. But, in an atmosphere that is both hotter than the body and saturated with water vapor, even heat loss by evaporation is ineffective. It should be noted that there is always some heat loss by evaporation, even if the animal is not actively sweating. For example, the respiratory gases are saturated with water vapor, and much of this is expelled during each exhalation. In addition, there is always a loss of water from the skin in the form of "insensible perspiration," so called because there is no obvious beading of water on the surface which generally accompanies active sweating. In a dry hot desert, particularly if the wind is blowing, there may not be any outward sign of sweating in spite of the fact that relatively large amounts of water are being excreted. Under such conditions, an active adult human could lose more than 3 liters of water per hour. It is apparent that without replacement of this water, one could become rapidly dehydrated.

As a first approximation, sweat consists of an altered ultrafiltrate of plasma, ranging in NaCl content from about 1/10 that of plasma to an almost equal concentration. It contains about the same concentrations of potassium, urea and lactic acid as plasma, with smaller amounts of glucose and amino acids. Therefore it is also possible to realize a considerable salt loss as a result of profuse sweating, especially if it is prolonged and only the water deficit is replenished.

Many mammals and birds and at least some reptiles utilize the panting reflex when overheated. In this process, air moved rapidly over the oral and respiratory membranes enhances the evaporation rate. During panting, the ventilation movements are sufficiently shallow to prevent an appreciable increase in gas exchange in the alveoli and the consequent removal of too much CO_2. Such shallow ventilation is necessary, because, when the CO_2 tension of the body fluids is lowered, there is a loss of acid and an increase in the alkalinity of the tissues.

An impressive demonstration of thermostat activity is observed during the course of fever. There are many fever-producing substances (generally called pyrogens) that are capable of resetting the hypothalamic thermostat to a higher level. These are often foreign proteins or protein byproducts that are sometimes present during infections. When the reference temperature of the thermostat is abruptly raised, the victim feels cold, the blood vessels of the skin contract, shivering occurs and the general heat gain processes are mobilized. Once the body temperature reaches the new elevated thermostat setting it remains at the fever level as long as the reference temperature is also elevated. When the pyrogen is removed and the thermostat resets itself to its original level, the body temperature is then higher than the reference setting. As a result, the heat loss mechanisms such as skin vessel dilation and sweating are activated until normal body temperature is reached.

EFFECTS OF EXTREME ENVIRONMENTS

A major cause of tissue damage and death due to severe cold exposure is the formation of ice in the tissues. However, several organisms, including small mammals, have survived rapid experimental cooling to below 0°C. Under these carefully controlled conditions, supercooling rather than ice formation is achieved, and the animals have been brought back to normal body temperatures with little damage. Following cold exposure which is severe enough to lower the body temperature from 37°C to about 33°C, the human hypothalamus begins to fail as a regulator. By the time the temperature of the interior of the body has reached 25-27°C essentially no regulation is occurring. Anesthesia sets in at this point and the body temperature falls rapidly. In severe cold, the extremities tend to freeze even though the core temperature may remain near 37°C. This is due to the normal closure of the superficial blood vessels which retards heat loss by radiation.

In all homeothermic animals there is a range of environmental temperature within which the body temperature can be regulated at a constant level by the "radiator system," that is, by the skin perfusion reflex and by the adjustments of fur or plumage. This range, generally called the *thermoneutral zone*, depends upon the relative effectiveness of the insulation. For example, it includes the environmental temperature range from approximately 26°C to 31°C for a nude man, but the addition of clothing can extend this range considerably. For an arctic fox or a husky, the lower end of the range may be −30°C. Outside of the thermoneutral zone, shivering and sweating are required to maintain the body temperature. During prolonged cold exposure, the metabolism is increased to compensate for heat loss; this response requires a secretion of the thyroid gland. Some evidence suggests that the level of the thyroid secretion is controlled by the hypothalamus, presumably as part of its normal thermostat function.

At very high heat loads, both the heat-dissipating mechanisms and the thermostat of homeotherms fail. When this happens, the metabolic rate increases according to the Q_{10} rule and the body temperature rises rapidly. The complications of serious overheating are manifold. Since the evaporation of water becomes a major avenue of cooling, dehydration occurs quickly, and fluids are withdrawn from the plasma resulting in a hemoconcentration (thickening of the blood and plasma). This in turn overworks the heart, and impairs circulation to the kidneys and the capillaries. There is generally a salt imbalance accompanying profuse sweating which adds its complications. In addition, the central nervous system of most mammals may suffer permanent damage following a 10-12°C rise in body temperature.

In summary, the thermostat of homeotherms is useful in a relatively narrow range of body temperature. The control mechanisms are able to maintain relatively constant internal temperatures within a wide range of environmental temperatures, especially if the organism is well insulated. In the thermoneutral zones, there is a minimal rate of metabolism. In the homeotherms, this basal rate increases at temperatures below the thermoneutral zone, and also at higher body temperatures, particularly when the thermostat itself fails to function properly.

OTHER TEMPERATURE RESPONSES

Although poikilotherms, by definition, regulate their body temperature poorly, they nevertheless possess some excellent temperature receptors. Some of these are apparently skin receptors which are instrumental in seeking out tolerable environmental temperatures. In a well-defined temperature gradient, certain fish will repeatedly select an area which differs from their immediate surroundings by only a few tenths of a degree centigrade. Other examples include: a. bees which fan their hive when it reaches a certain critical temperature, usually 35°C; b. reptiles and some insects whose basking behaviors are related to fairly sensitive general temperature senses; c. certain blood-sucking organisms, including insects, which locate their prey, at least in part, by a temperature sense combined with an acute chemical sense.

Some of the most phenomenal temperature receptors in the animal kingdom are those of the pit vipers, such as the rattlesnakes. These snakes generally have poor vision and are often nocturnal. They prey largely upon warm-blooded animals whose body temperature is higher than that of the snake itself or the surroundings. It has been shown by T. H. Bullock and his colleagues that the pit receptor surface consists of many free nerve endings on a thin membrane situated immediately in front of a tissue gas space. These workers also found that the receptor endings respond to extremely small changes in temperature of the membrane — of the order of only 0.003°C. Warm-blooded prey, such as small mammals or birds, radiate heat in the form of infrared at wave lengths between 0.5 and about 20 microns. The pit receptors are sensitive in the range from about 1.5 to 15 microns. It is estimated that a rattlesnake can detect an object in his environment that differs no more than 0.1°C from the surroundings. The pits, like the eyes, have a defined "field of view." The field, however, is not determined by lenses, but by the fact that the receptor membrane is situated at the rear of the pit in such a manner that the walls cast shadows for infrared coming from the periphery. The animal therefore "sees" two cones of infrared which overlap somewhat in the center of the field. Since other distance senses such as vision and hearing are relatively poor in these animals, the pits represent the major sensory input for the detection of prey.

Certain reptiles exhibit special behavioral mechanisms, such as basking in the sun, seeking shade, burrowing or panting, which aid in maintaining relatively constant temperatures. Most poikilotherms, moreover, do not attempt to maintain activity during severely cold weather, but seek instead a secluded and insulated spot in which to overwinter. Fish, for example, migrate to portions of their stream which do not freeze. Frogs spend most of the coldest part of the winter in the water or mud of a pond or stream. Toads often burrow to appreciable depths in the soil, even to several feet in high latitudes, to avoid the frost line. Insects overwinter in the egg, embryonic, larval or pupal stages in the soil or in streams or ponds, or they go into a state of torpor in some protected place. It is apparent that activity regulation and events such as reproduction must be under the control of some "biological clock" mechanism, integrated with environmental cues such as day length and ambient temperature.

A number of novel mechanisms have evolved which increase chances of survival in harsh environments. Some unicellular organisms undergo marked dehydration, which presumably limits the free water available for freezing. Certain moths and wasps actually synthesize an antifreeze, glycerol, which lowers the freezing point of their tissues sufficiently to prevent ice formation. Similar accumulations of tolerable metabolites may occur in a number of different organisms as a mechanism of adaptation to severe cold or intense heat.

HIBERNATION

Among a number of mammals and a few birds, hibernation, or overwintering in a dormant state, has evolved as a means of surviving the cold and the decreased food supply. There is no clear knowledge of the conditions which initiate hibernation, nor is there an explanation for the termination of the state. The physiological characteristics of the state, however, are well documented for a number of typical hibernators such as bats, hamsters, ground squirrels, and woodchucks.

Although the hibernating state is variable among different species, it generally includes some or all of the following: The insulin level is often elevated thus producing a correspondingly low blood sugar level. Depressed thyroid activity helps to provide a metabolic rate that is only a fraction of that of the active animal. In most hibernators the thermostat is so affected that body temperature is allowed to approach that of the surroundings. There is usually an accumulation of fat, including a characteristic "brown fat." Except for a few species such as the hamster, metabolic fuel is largely derived from body fat that was accumulated prior to the onset of hibernation. Finally there are some changes in the plasma composition including an increased concentration of magnesium, an ion which has an anesthetic effect.

Insulin injections alone are effective in inducing hibernation in some animals, e.g., the hedgehog, but not in others. Perhaps the most nearly universal inducer is the lowering of the environmental temperature, particularly in conjunction with a diminishing photoperiod.

At the onset of hibernation there is not an immediate fall in body temperature, but rather a gradual lowering in stages called "test drops" which occur over a period of several days. Each test drop is initiated by a general skin vasodilation which promotes heat dissipation by radiation to the environment. This is usually accompanied by a marked lowering of both muscular tone and metabolic rate. These responses are probably under control of the central nervous system, specifically the hypothalamus. At each test drop, the body temperature falls 5-10°C, but usually returns to normal within a few hours. Although each successive drop is lower and more prolonged, most hibernators do not remain in cold torpor for more than about a week at a time. Hamsters, for example, arouse every few days and may feed, defecate and urinate. Some bats remain in torpor for more than a month between spontaneous arousals, but this is unusual for hibernators in general.

Hibernators are not true poikilotherms during torpor, although their body temperatures may actually reach ambient levels. There remains a degree of temperature regulation, as if the thermostat were set much lower than normal. Severe cold exposure, for example, usually increases metabolism and causes arousal. Likewise, a warming of the environment is effective in producing arousal.

Arousal from hibernation is accompanied by an activation of the usual heat-gain mechanisms. Typically there is a skin vasoconstriction and a violent shivering. The heart itself becomes more active and adds significant amounts of heat. Most importantly, it has been shown recently that the characteristic brown fat deposits are particularly thermogenic during arousal, but the mechanism controlling the metabolic processes in these tissues is poorly understood. Prior to the final termination of hibernation there is a reestablishment of endocrine balance, including a diminished level of insulin and an increase in the amount of thyroxin.

The question of regulation of cyclical hibernation activity is of particular importance. The onset of hibernation does not always depend upon the availability of food, nor even upon the environmental temperature. Even in conjunction with day length, these factors do not entirely explain the cyclic activity. For example, woodchucks generally become very fat and enter hibernation while the weather is still fairly warm and while food is still in abundance. In addition, they may arouse completely and leave their burrows while it is still cold. In fact, they may be seen early in the spring while there is still snow and almost no food available. During deep hibernation most of these animals are insulated from the usual environmental cues of temperature and day length. Bats, for example, often hibernate in caves in perpetual darkness where the mean environmental temperature is almost constant throughout the year. It is theorized that these animals possess an internal, biological clock which regulates hibernation activity, but the nature of such a clock remains unknown.

References

BLUM, F. H., *Time's Arrow and Evolution*, 2nd ed. New York: Harper, 1962.

KLEIBER, MAX, *The Fire of Life; An Introduction to Animal Energetics*, New York: John Wiley and Sons, Inc., 1961.

LEHNINGER, A. L., *Bioenergetics*, New York: W. A. Benjamin, Inc., 1965.

SCHMIDT-NIELSEN, K., *Desert Animals: Physiological Problems of Heat and Water*. Oxford: Clarendon Press, 1964.

WHITE, A., HANDLER, P., and SMITH, E. L., *Principles of Biochemistry*, 3rd ed. New York: McGraw-Hill Book Co., 1964. Ch. 16.

CHAPTER 7

Muscle

INTRODUCTION

Because of their peculiar contractile properties, muscle cells are capable of shortening and exerting tension on their attachments. The individual cells are combined into larger structural units, the muscles, which work in concert, moving various parts of the organism as directed by the nervous and endocrine systems. In all, muscle tissues of a typical mammal amount to about forty per cent of the total body weight. Skeletal muscle, which is under voluntary control, undergoes remarkable changes in metabolic rate in relatively short periods of time. Consequently, when considering muscle, one must bear in mind the complexity of the nervous control, the energy expenditure, the circulation and temperature changes, as well as the metabolic transfer involved in the normal function of this large tissue mass.

The intent of this chapter is to focus attention first on the organization of muscle cells, particularly with reference to such key structures as excitable membranes, contractile proteins, and the nerve supply. An effort is then made to relate these and other aspects of morphology to the overall function of muscles. In order to show how alternative means of performing common types of movement have evolved, examples have been incorporated from a variety of animals. Finally a short section is given on a special function of muscle tissue, the production of electricity.

STRUCTURE OF MUSCLE

Striated muscle fibers are relatively large cells, 10-100 microns in diameter and varying in length from a few millimeters up to several centimeters. Each fiber is encased in a delicate connective tissue sheath called the endomysium which carries one or two capillaries along its length. The larger blood vessels course along the connective tissues ensheathing the fiber bundles or fasiculi. The encasing connective tissue of the major bundles extends beyond them to connect with tendons or fascia which in turn are attached to the periosteum of the bones. Each individual muscle fiber contains several peripherally located nuclei suspended in the sarcoplasm (cytoplasm). Toward the center of the cell are numerous tightly packed contractile elements, the *myofibrils*. Scattered throughout the sarcoplasm, or oriented with relation to the myofibrils, are the muscle mitochondria or sarcosomes, which synthesize ATP. All of these organelles are surrounded by a complex plasma membrane or *sarcolemma*. Finally, associated with the sarcolemma of each fiber is an axon branch from a motor neuron which forms a special synaptic terminal called a *myoneural junction*.

The interesting and complex arrangement of contractile elements one finds within skeletal muscle fibers is shown diagrammatically in Figs. 7-1 — 7-3. The most striking gross structural features of the cell, the striations, are actually derived from the subcellular myofibrils. The repeating light and dark bands are divided into *sarcomeres,* the units bounded by the Z lines. Since the Z lines are in register in all of the myofibrils of the fiber, the striated pattern is imposed on the whole cell. Electron microscopy has revealed an ultrastructure in these striations which is central to the current theory of muscular contraction. There are two filamentous arrays present in the sarcomere which interdigitate (Fig. 7-2). While the thin filaments are anchored at the Z lines, the thick filaments are suspended between the thin ones with bridge-like projections toward the latter (Fig. 7-3). The functional significance of this organization will be described below.

Smooth muscles are characteristically located around the hollow organs of the body. They form the contractile portions of the gastrointestinal tract, the blood vessels (except the capillaries) the walls of the ureter, bladder, genital system and bronchioles of the lungs. Smooth muscles are also found in the ducts of most glands, the ciliary body and iris of the eye and in the piloerector apparatus. Classically, smooth muscle cells are shown as spindle shaped, and most are of this type. However, they may also be irregularly shaped or even stellate. There is usually a single nucleus, along with mitochondria and the usual additional cell inclusions. Their contractile elements appear as delicate fibrils of nearly uniform size. Cross striation or other evidence of differentiation within the fibrils has not been described. Smooth muscles are innervated from one or both divisions of the autonomic nervous system. Although there is considerable variation, each cell usually receives several motor neuron terminals, however, some cells receive none.

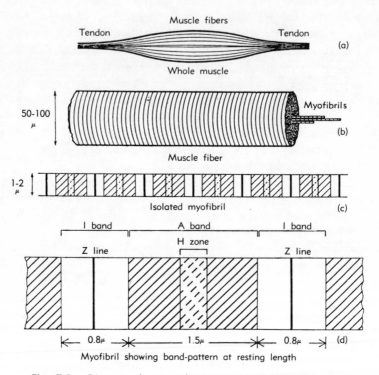

Fig. 7-1. Diagram showing the position and arrangement of fibers and fibrils in vertebrate skeletal muscle. In (a), the whole muscle, made up of muscle fibers (cells). (b) Shows the manner in which the sub-cellular myofibrils are arranged within a single cell. The striations in skeletal muscle are imposed by the repeating light and dark bands of the myofibrils (c). The dimensions and appearance of these striations are shown in (d). The minimal functional unit, the sarcomere, is bounded by the **Z** lines. Electron microscopy has revealed finer details in the myofibril (Fig. 7-2) including the protein filaments and their attachments. (From H. E. Huxley and J. Hanson, "The Molecular Bases of Contraction in Cross-striated Muscle." Ch. VII., Vol. I., **The Structure and Function of Muscle.** G. Bourne, ed. Academic Press, New York, 1960.)

Vertebrate cardiac muscle in certain aspects resembles both skeletal and smooth muscle. Striations similar to those described for skeletal muscle are present, including Z, A and I bands. As do smooth muscle fibers, cardiac muscle cells generally have only a single nucleus. They are of course spontaneously active like many smooth muscles, and are controlled by autonomic fibers in a similar manner. The most striking feature

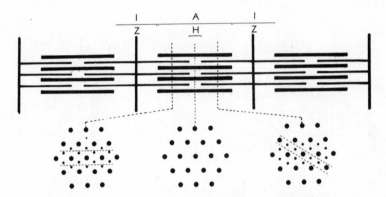

Fig. 7-2. Diagram reconstructed from an electron micrograph, showing the organization of thick and thin filaments of myofibrils. Compare the striations with those in (d) of Fig. 7-1. The lower portion of the figure shows the appearance of thick and thin filaments taken in cross-section at three points along the **A** and **H** bands. This indicates that the thick filaments are suspended between the thin filaments. The bridges which attach the two are not shown (however see Fig. 7-3). (From H. E. Huxley and J. Hanson, "The Molecular Basis of Contraction in Cross-striated Muscle." Ch. VII., Vol. I, **The Structure and Function of Muscle.** G. Bourne, ed. Academic Press, New York, 1960.)

of cardiac muscle is the presence of *intercalated discs* between the cells. Until recently, cardiac muscle was considered to be a syncytium. This was a reasonable assumption from the evidence of light microscopy and from the fact that an all-or-none contraction phenomenon is characteristic of heart muscle. Recent studies with the electron microscope, however, revealed that the individual cells are in fact separate and bordered by a typical sarcolemma. Cardiac cells are richly supplied with mitochondria and contain considerable quantities of glycogen and fat as well. A dense capillary bed is present which is derived from the coronary arteries.

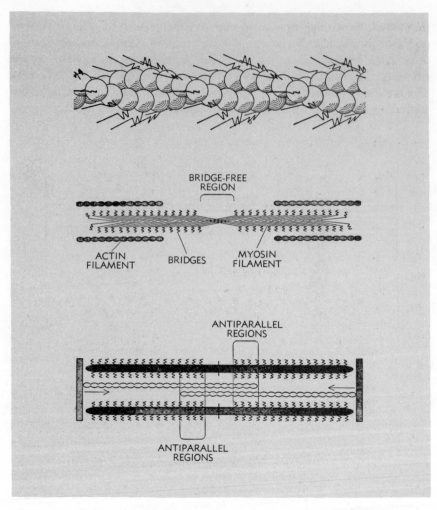

BRIDGE-FREE
REGION

ACTIN   MYOSIN
FILAMENT   BRIDGES   FILAMENT

ANTIPARALLEL
REGIONS

ANTIPARALLEL
REGIONS

Fig. 7-3. Diagram to illustrate the bridges projecting from the thick toward the thin filaments in a myofibril. The information required for these reconstructions was obtained from electron microscopy, protein chemistry and x-ray diffraction. The upper diagram shows a coiled strand of protein representing a thin actin filament with an arrangement of myosin bridge attachments. The middle figure shows how individual myosin molecules are arranged to form the thick filament. The projecting portion of each myosin molecule which forms a bridge also functions as an ATP-ase (see text). The lower diagram shows a sarcomere at maximum shortening. Here, the actin (thin) filaments overlap somewhat preventing an efficient attachment of the myosin bridges (antiparallel regions). The greatest tension is attained therefore when the actin filaments approach each other in the **H** zone. (From H. E. Huxley, "The Mechanism of Muscular Contraction." **Scientific American** Dec., 1965.)

CONTRACTILE PROTEINS

The myofibrils of skeletal muscle are composed largely of three proteins which are associated to form the contractile apparatus proper. They are called *actin, myosin* and *tropomyosin.* Each protein has a different solubility in neutral KCl solutions; a property which has allowed them to be purified and characterized chemically. Pure myosin has enzymatic activity as an ATPase. This activity is enhanced if actin is present also. Furthermore, gelled threads composed of actin and myosin will actually contract if ATP is added in the presence of appropriate ions. Such threads, however, contract very slowly and fail to exert any appreciable tension, presumably because the proteins are not properly oriented. If one extracts a thin strip of muscle with 50% glycerol, one can remove the more soluble proteins but retain the less soluble contractile proteins in their proper orientation. If one then adds ATP and appropriate ions, the "glycerol-extracted" muscle will respond with a slow but strong contraction. The failure of such models to contract rapidly is due primarily to the absence of the cell membrane and the accompanying activation system typical of living muscle.

Actin is known to be a major component of the thin filaments while myosin is localized in the thick filaments in vertebrate skeletal muscle. Tropomyosin, on the other hand, is present in both the Z membranes and the thin filaments. The function of tropomyosin is not as well understood as is that of actin or myosin; however, from the quantity and location of this protein, it too must have a central role in the contraction process.

Contractile proteins typical of skeletal muscles are also present in smooth and cardiac muscle, although their arrangement into functional elements is different. In fact, many cells, both motile and non-motile, contain various amounts of actin- and myosin-like proteins. Such processes as amoeboid movement, ciliary motion, cyclosis and even cell division may be related basically to muscle contraction through the interaction of common contractile proteins.

THE SLIDING FILAMENT MODEL OF VERTEBRATE SKELETAL MUSCLE

The current theory for the mechanism of contraction of vertebrate skeletal muscle is based upon considerable evidence that the thick and thin filaments of the myofibrils slide past one another in the process of shortening. The energy coupling is assumed to be by way of the myosin bridges which extend outward to contact the actin filaments. The diagram of Fig. 7-3 conveys the basic notions. Here, the minimal functional unit for contraction may be considered as the individual sarcomere, or the segment between successive Z lines.

It should be noted that the length of the thick myosin and thin actin filaments remains constant while the strands interdigitate. Examination of single living muscle fibers shows therefore, a constant length A band and a diminishing I band during contraction. Similarly, stretching of the muscle also shows a constant length A band, but an increase in the length of the I band. This is consistent with the assumption that the filaments remain unfolded and slide past one another.

It is further assumed that the force which directs the sliding is imparted by the attachment and rotation of the bridges which extend from the thick filaments outward to the thin filaments (Fig. 7-3). By some means, the free energy of the phosphate bonds of ATP is transferred to the myosin bridges during the attachment and rotation process. Although the mechanism is not clear in detail, it is presumably the central energy transformation involved in muscle contraction.

Although the sliding model is based largely on studies of ultrastructure, it is consistent with several basic physiological properties of skeletal muscle. For example, it is known that an inverse relationship exists between the velocity of contraction and the tension which can be exerted. From the model presented, one could imagine that during very rapid contractions perhaps all of the available bridge attachments and rotations could not be made, thus diminishing the tension exerted. Second, it has long been known that a muscle requires energy to shorten whether or not it is lifting a load, i.e., doing external work. In fact, the total energy required for the shortening phase is the sum of the energy of activation, the work done, and the *distance moved*. It is reasonably assumed that for each myosin bridge which attaches and rotates, a certain amount of energy is expended. Since the bridges are linearly oriented in the direction of contraction, the further the muscle contracts, the more bridges must be formed and the more energy must be expended.

ACTIVATION OF CONTRACTION

Skeletal muscles are ordinarily activated only upon receiving signals from the motor nerves. Several events are involved in this process as indicated by the following sequence: a. nerve spike arrives at its terminal → b. acetylocholine (Acch) released from nerve terminal → c. Acch diffuses to muscle membrane → d. Acch activates muscle membrane → e. muscle spike potential-activation of contractile elements by calcium release → and f. muscle contraction. In the vertebrate skeletal muscle fiber, this process is generally all-or-none. If a spike potential arrives from a motor nerve, the other processes follow reliably, resulting in a complete contraction cycle.

There is a space between the nerve and the muscle, perhaps 200 Angstroms wide. Acetylcholine is a *neurotransmitter*, functioning to transfer the excitation across this space from the motor nerve membrane to the muscle fiber membrane. Acetylocholine is synthesized by the nerve and stored until released, at which point, it diffuses rapidly toward the muscle membrane, attaches at specific sites, and initiates excitation in the muscle by altering membrane permeability to surrounding ions. The events of the muscle spike are essentially the same as those in nerve trunks. Synaptic transmission between nerve and muscle is also similar to nerve-nerve transmission. Because of these similarities, the details of the excitation process will be deferred to the chapter which follows.

The mechanism which allows the excitation of the membrane to activate the contractile elements of muscle cells is poorly understood. Some information is available, however, concerning the conduction of the excitation from the surface membrane to the cell interior. In the case of vertebrate skeletal muscle, there are numerous infoldings of the external membrane which form a complex transverse *sarcotubular system*. These in turn are connected by similar delicate tubules that run longitudinally between the myofibrils inside the cell. Significantly, these two tubular systems join at the Z membranes of each sarcomere of the myofibrils. It is known that the threshold for electrical stimulation is lowest when current is applied near the Z lines of single muscle fibers. It is thought therefore that the inward foldings of the membrane conduct the impulse toward the center of the cell to the region of the Z membranes. The rapid spread of the spike potential over the surface of the cell (conduction velocity about 5 meters/second) is transferred inward equally as fast by the tubular system. In this way, the entire cell is able to contract at once because each sarcomere shortens essentially at the same time.

MOTOR UNITS AND GRADED CONTRACTIONS

Contractions must be graded in both force and velocity in order to insure smooth and controlled movements under varying loads. Such gradations must be accomplished in spite of the all-or-none response typical of individual muscle fibers.

The all-or-none contraction which is observed in skeletal muscle in response to a single threshold stimulus is called a *twitch*. This is a rapid event that is complete usually within 15 to 100 milliseconds in various muscles. The electrical events of the muscle membrane are even faster and are generally complete within about 5 milliseconds. One could expect, therefore, to be able to trigger repetitively the electrical activity of the membrane fast enough to "fuse" the mechanical contractions. Such a fusion in fact does occur upon rapid repetitive stimulation causing the muscle to shorten and remain in a contracted state called *tetany*.

Each motoneuron supplies nerve terminals to hundreds or even thousands of muscle fibers. The cell bodies of the motoneurons are located in the ventral portion of the spinal grey matter. Each motoneuron and its associated muscle fibers form a *motor unit* (Fig. 7-4). Since the whole motor unit functions in an all-or-none manner, each spike in the motoneuron can be expected to produce a twitch in several hundred or thousand muscle cells. Each large anatomical unit, such as a major leg muscle, is made up of hundreds of thousands of muscle fibers, and is controlled by a few hundred motoneurons. The motoneurons involved in the activation of this leg muscle are associated synaptically with one another in the spinal cord, so that the control is exerted entirely from the central nervous system. In addition, these motoneurons are associated by means of interneurons with other motoneurons, for example those which control the opposing muscles in the leg.

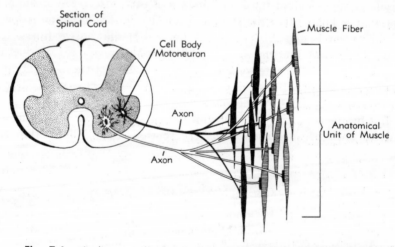

Fig. 7-4. A diagram illustrating two motor units within a muscle. Each motor unit is composed of one motoneuron and its associated muscle fibers. Each neuron may control from a few dozen to several thousand muscle cells, depending upon the requirements for precision of movement.

The grading of contraction is achieved by two means: first, by the selection and number of motor units active, and second by the frequency of firing of the active motor units. Most motoneurons fire in bursts, rather than in single spikes. There is a wide frequency range of firing available, anywhere from a few spikes per second, giving a few twitches per second, to a high frequency which is capable of tetanizing all of the muscle fibers of that motor unit. During prolonged contraction of a large muscle, the various motor units are activated alternately in a manner that can maintain the contraction, and avoid fatigue. In order to exert maximal tension under large loads, virtually all the motor units may be mobilized simultaneously, with firings in the motoneurons at tetanizing frequencies.

The decision is made in the central nervous system to activate a certain motor unit; thousands of neurons cooperate in this decision. Some of them are localized in the spinal cord, others in various parts of the brain. The sensory information required for this decision is obtained in part from the muscles themselves. Within each bundle of muscles, and also associated with the tendon attachments, are special receptors which inform the central nervous system of the force on the muscle attachments, as well as the rate and the extent of stretch. Additional important sensory information is obtained from the equilibrium centers of the inner ear and from the visual system. Through a complex integration, we are able to command a certain movement and to compare our commands with the actual results through sensory feedback. More details concerning this integration will be given in the two chapters which follow.

As one would expect, some muscles require a more precise control than others. It is apparent that a more refined gradation and control could be exerted by a muscle if the motor units were small and numerous. This relationship is actually found in the vertebrate system. For instance, the muscles that control the accurate movements of the eyeball, or those of the hands and face, which also perform delicate movements, generally possess small motor units of perhaps less than a hundred fibers each. In contrast, the postural muscles of the trunk, which function mainly to simply support the animal against gravity, typically have motor units composed of thousands of muscle fibers.

SKELETAL MUSCLE ACTIVATION IN THE INVERTEBRATES

For the most part, the mode of activation of skeletal muscle in invertebrates is entirely different from that just described for vertebrates. The vertebrate system, although the most familiar to us, actually represents a special case when the broad spectrum of muscle types is considered. Briefly, let us compare the innervation and activation of the skeletal muscle fibers of a vertebrate, a crustacean and an insect (Fig. 7-5). The motor nerves supplying a crustacean or an insect skeletal muscle fiber generally end in many fine terminals (polyterminal) rather than in a single myoneural junction typical of the vertebrate skeletal muscles.

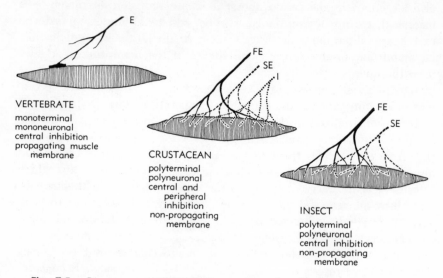

Fig. 7-5. Diagram comparing the innervation of a vertebrate, a crustacean and an insect skeletal muscle fiber. The letter (E) indicates the single excitor fiber typical of vertebrate fast skeletal muscle. (FE) and (SE) represent fast and slow excitor fibers, while (I) indicates a peripheral inhibitor.

In addition, the arthropod muscles often receive several nerve supplies to a single muscle cell (polyneuronal). One or more of these are generally *fast excitors* (FE) and the others are *slow excitors* (SE). Crustacean skeletal muscles often receive the terminals of an additional axon, the inhibitor (I). Neither vertebrate nor most insect skeletal muscles receive a peripheral inhibitor. In general, the membranes of the muscle fibers of the arthropods do not exhibit the propagating spike potentials typical of vertebrate skeletal muscle fibers. The polyterminal endings are therefore needed in arthropod muscle to elicit a uniform excitation over the surface. The fast axons elicit a rapid twitch-like contraction while the slow axons give a slow or sustained contraction. They may accomplish this by releasing different transmitters at their terminals. In the crustacean, stimulation of the inhibitor axon may either diminish or abolish the action of the excitor axons, while in vertebrates and in most insects, inhibition is achieved centrally (in the central nervous system) by suppression of excitability of the motoneurons themselves. Grading of contraction is achieved in arthropod skeletal muscle by the selective activation of either the fast or the slow axons. Further gradation can be realized by firing either the central and/or peripheral inhibitors. Finally, by changing the frequency of firing in the motor and inhibitor axons, both force and rate of contraction can be varied in a manner comparable to that in the vertebrates.

Many unique and interesting examples of muscle activation are known from the invertebrates. One of the more striking cases involves the "indirect flight," or "fibrillar," muscles which drive the wings of dipteran and hymenopteran insects.

The flight muscles of grasshoppers (Order Orthoptera) and butterflies (Order Lepidoptera) are attached directly between the wings and the exoskeleton. The frequency of wing beat in these insects is relatively fast, being of the order of 20 strokes per second, but not too fast to be accounted for by conventional neuronal activation. Wing movements of other insects, such as flies, midges, mosquitoes (Order Diptera) or bees and wasps (Order Hymenoptera), however, are extremely rapid, typically 200 to 300 strokes per second and, in a few species, as high as 1000 per second. Each muscle contraction here cannot be driven by a corresponding nerve spike for several reasons. First, these muscles, like most others, will tetanize when stimulated at frequencies of 50 to 70 per second. Second, the highest contraction frequencies can often exceed the upper firing frequency for the motor nerves themselves. Fibrillar muscles must be able, therefore, to contract several times for each spike which arrives from the motor nerves. The intervening contractions between the activating impulses appear to be induced by stretch.

The muscles themselves are attached indirectly to the wings through the resilient exoskeleton. There are two sets, one oriented dorsoventrally (DV), the other longitudinally (L) (Fig. 7-6). In principle, the contraction of one set of muscles distorts the skeleton and stretches the opposing set of muscles. The opposing muscles then become activated and contract. As each opposing muscle group contracts alternately the skeleton thus bends and recoils to drive the wings indirectly. Not every wing beat is accompanied by a spike, so the active state must be maintained for periods of several beats while the quick stretch and release keeps the contractions going. At high frequencies, there is apparently a delay between the length change and the tension change; this allows stretch,

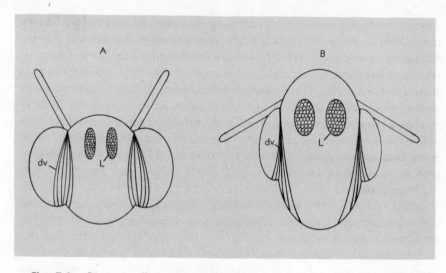

Fig. 7-6. Diagram illustrating how the contractions of indirect flight muscles produce distortions of the skeleton that result in wing movements. (L) the dorsal longitudinal muscles; (dv) dorsoventral muscles. In (A) the dorsoventral muscles are contracted causing the lever system of the skeleton to lift the wings. When the skeleton is in this position the dorsal longitudinal muscles are stretched. The rapid stretch of the L muscles results in their contraction as in (B) which in turn forces the wings down. In this position, the dv muscles are stretched causing the cycle to be repeated (see text).

but subsequently produces tension. According to this scheme, the prolonged active state, the built-in delay and the sensitivity to stretch appear to be key features of these unusual muscles. The elasticity of the muscles and exoskeleton insure that the whole system oscillates at its resonant frequency. As one would expect, therefore, clipping or loading the wings has a tendency to raise or lower the frequency of wing oscillation. For example, frequencies as high as 1000 cycles/second have been obtained after clipping the wings of small flies.

CONTRACTION IN SMOOTH AND CARDIAC MUSCLE

The movements of the intestine, heart and blood vessels are relatively slow in comparison with those of the skeleton. Smooth and cardiac muscles function by changing the size of the blood vessels (to alter resistance to blood flow) and by exerting pressure on the internal contents of the hollow organs (pumping action of the heart or the propulsion of intestinal contents). Several special properties have evolved in smooth and cardiac muscle which help perform these tasks. Consider first the case of cardiac muscle. If tetany routinely occurred in the heart every time a burst of spikes was received from the regulator nerves, its usefulness as a pump would be poor. Even though heart muscle can be tetanized under special conditions, normally there is a long *refractory period* following each contraction which renders the tissue relatively inexcitable. Consequently, there is a characteristic pause in activity which insures regularly paced contractions. A second important characteristic is reflected in the stretch response. Since the strength of the heart beat increases in proportion to the extent of filling, a local mechanism is provided by the muscle itself which helps to regulate the overall cardiac output.

Both smooth and cardiac muscles may contract spontaneously and even rhythmically without extrinsic nervous activation, but the rate and strength of the contractions are ordinarily controlled by the nervous system. The innervation, however, is *autonomic* and control is therefore involuntary. Since each muscle cell may not receive a nerve ending, the transmission of excitation through a layer of smooth or cardiac muscle is achieved largely by direct conduction from muscle cell to adjacent cell. In the intestine, a contraction may be initiated spontaneously, by stretch, or by local nerve stimulation. Once initiated, it spreads along the intestinal wall forcing the contents ahead of the contraction wave. There is a local nerve plexus in the wall of the intestine which coordinates the activities of the longitudinal and circular muscle layers. Two types of contractions characterize visceral smooth muscle. There are slow alternate cycles of contraction and relaxation called rhythmic contractions, and there is a slower sustained shortening which is referred to as a tonic contraction. The rhythmic waves may be superimposed on the slower tonic contractions.

Varying degrees of dependency upon nerve activation are seen in smooth muscles. The muscles which control pupillary diameter, for example, are almost totally dependent upon nervous activation and control. Intestinal muscle is somewhat independent of its nerve supply for initiation of contraction but is dependent upon it for control. Uterine muscle, in contrast, is relatively independent of nervous activation and control, but is responsive to several hormones including estrogen, progesterone, oxytocin and vasopressin. The latter hormones stimulate several types of smooth muscles, but those of the uterus and blood vessels are most susceptible. The most universally effective hormones in controlling both smooth and cardiac muscle are norepinephrine and epinephrine from the adrenal medulla. Depending upon the muscle, the effects of norepinephrine and epinephrine may be either excitatory (constricts the blood vessels of the skin and intestine) or inhibitory (diminishes contractility of the intestine and bronchioles as well as the blood vessels of the heart and skeletal muscles).

It is of interest to note that the innervation of certain types of smooth muscles of the vertebrates, particularly the visceral muscles, is similar to that described for arthropod skeletal muscle. Typically, both excitatory and inhibitory fibers are supplied from the sympathetic and parasympathetic branches of the autonomic nervous system. Even polyterminal endings are found occasionally, although neighboring cells may not be innervated. The motor unit concept does not strictly apply to either the vertebrate visceral muscle or the arthropod skeletal fibers. Arthropod muscle differs from vertebrate visceral muscle in the important respect that the former is not spontaneously active, but as noted above, even the smooth muscles are not universally autogenic.

SPECIALIZED MUSCLE: ELECTRIC ORGANS

A number of fishes have evolved electric organs from muscle tissue or from myoneural junctions. Some of these are capable of producing impressive voltages (fresh-water forms such as the electric eel, *Electrophorus electricus*) or enormous currents (marine species such as the elasmobranch *Torpedo*). Electric fish use these weapons to stun prey and to ward off their enemies, and if applied under certain conditions, these electric shocks can be lethal, even for animals as large as man.

How is electricity generated in these organs? The modified muscle cells (called electroplaques) of various electric organs show considerable variations in morphology. Generally they are thin flat cells that are packed together in various ways. In most fish, only one side of each electroplaque is innervated, and all of the innervated surfaces usually face in the same direction. The membranes of electroplaques, like those of other muscle cells, are polarized (+) outside and (−) inside at about 0.08 volts (80 millivolts). Upon activation from motoneurons, the innervated sides undergo a depolarization to zero and beyond until the cell interior is about +65 mv (Fig. 7-7). Meanwhile, the polarity of the non-innervated side of the electroplaque remains unchanged. Thus a potential of about 0.15 volts is generated by each electroplaque as a result of adding the potentials across the two sides.

How do such small potentials, generated by the individual electroplaque, contribute to the powerful voltages and currents typical of the whole electric organ? The two organs of the electric eel, *Electrophorus electricus*, have about 5,000 to 10,000 electroplaques serially arranged

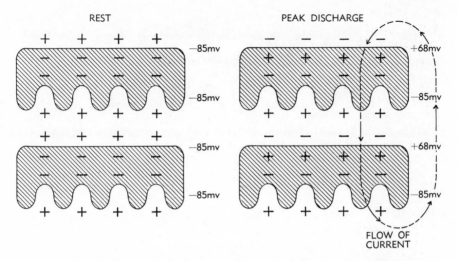

Fig. 7-7. Electrical changes associated with the electroplaques of the eel, **Electrophorus.** At rest, the two plaques are polarized in the conventional manner. During activity, the caudal faces of the plates undergo the reversal of charge (positive inside) that is typical of spike overshoots. As a result, the plates in series add the polarized voltage. Low resistance of the non-innervated face rostral allows current flow as shown.

into about 70 parallel columns. The two electric organs account for about 40 per cent of the mass of the animal's body. When thousands of such electroplaques are arranged in series, the total voltage is additive, just as it is when one arranges batteries in a series. Thus the electric eel with 5000 electroplaques in series could theoretically produce 750 volts, but due to some loss, they actually produce about 500 volts in each pulse. Such high voltages are thought to have evolved as a means of overcoming the high electrical resistance of the fresh-water environment. The marine species, *Torpedo,* has about 1000 electroplaques in each series and the discharge is correspondingly lower in voltage, but there are some 2000 such columns in parallel which provides an enormous amperage. Typically, *Torpedo* might discharge at 50 volts and 50 amperes, giving 2500 watts of power during a short pulse. The low voltages are adequate for conduction through ionized sea water, but in order to generate sufficient power, the pulses must be high in amperage.

All things considered, it really isn't so unusual for muscles to generate small electrical signals since they are all capable of doing so. The special aspects of electric organs which allow large voltages and currents are attributed to the behavior of the membranes and the arrangement of the cells into functional units.

REFERENCES

BOURNE, G. H., (ed.), *The Structures and Function of Muscle,* New York: Academic Press, 1960. Vol. I-III.

GRUNDFEST, H., "Electric Fishes." *Scientific American,* October, 1960, p. 115.

HOYLE, G., *Comparative Physiology of Nervous Control of Muscular Contraction,* Cambridge University Press, 1957.

HUXLEY, H. E., "The Contraction of Muscle." *Scientific American,* November, 1958, p. 66.

HUXLEY, H. E., "The Mechanism of Muscular Contraction." *Scientific American,* December, 1965, p. 18.

PORTER, K., and FRANZINI-ARMSTRONG, F., "The Sarcoplasmic Reticulum." *Scientific American,* March 1965, p. 72.

ROCKSTEIN, M., (ed.), *The Physiology of Insecta,* New York: Academic Press, 1965. Vol II, Ch. 6, 8.

SMITH, D. S., "The Flight Muscles of Insects." *Scientific American,* June, 1965, p. 76.

CHAPTER 8

Receptors
and sensory physiology

INTRODUCTION

The chapters which follow deal with the closely related topics of neurophysiology and endocrinology. The primary function of the combined sensory system is the gathering of information concerning the physical and chemical status of the internal and external environments. The nervous and endocrine systems integrate this incoming information along with that stored in the memory to coordinate the various parts of the body and to direct the reactions of the organism.

Receptors generally respond to a single type of stimulus, that is, temperature, pressure, chemicals, etc., and each neuron exhibits a range of response that is appropriate for the magnitude of change normally encountered. The evolution of this specificity, and range of response, probably came about as an extension of the basic irritable nature of nerve cells in general. For example, a response to temperature may be seen in most neurons, but those which have been specialized into receptors of heat or cold have a special sensitivity and range of their own. Most neurons also respond to chemicals, but not with the low thresholds or wide spectrum typical of true chemoreceptors. Similarly, mechanical distortion will stimulate most neurons, but the thresholds are high, or the response is too transient or too prolonged for them to function as useful mechanoreceptors.

The central nervous system is continually bombarded by hundreds of thousands of sensory signals. Filtration of the important signals from those of lesser urgency becomes a formidable task. Some properties of the receptors themselves help to limit the total amount of incoming information and to indicate the importance of the data being furnished. If a stimulus of constant intensity is applied for a prolonged period, the frequency of the response from a receptor is at first high, but then diminishes. This adaptation process is markedly different for the various types of receptors. While some are essentially non-adapting (pain), others may adapt almost completely in a few seconds (touch). A pain fiber that adapts before the damaging stimulus is removed, would defeat the purpose it serves. Similarly, a receptor which informs the central nervous system of extensor muscle tension during standing must be non-adapting. In contrast, a touch on the skin by a foreign object generally needs signalling only once, after which the receptor may adapt, even if the stimulus remains at its original intensity.

Sensory systems must be capable of responding to an enormous range of stimulus intensity. In addition, they must transmit this information to the central nervous system in an interpretable manner. Information is transmitted by impulses (also called spikes or action potentials) which are propagated along a neuron. The frequency of the spikes indicates the stimulus strength. Since the average receptor neuron is able to fire only at frequencies ranging from zero to about 500 spikes/second, they clearly are incapable of maintaining a linear response to stimulus strength that may vary in magnitude by a factor of a million or more. Receptors therefore respond to some fraction of the stimulus strength. By this mechanism, a meaningful signal can be coded for the large range of stimulus strength normally encountered.

EXCITATION AND PROPAGATION IN NEURONS

The initial process which takes place upon stimulation of a sensory neuron is the formation of a generator potential. This is a small non-propagated electrical charge which is the forerunner or "generator" of the large all-or-none propagated spike potential. Generator potentials may be thought of as small *voltage analogs* of some physical or chemical change which has occurred in the environment. They are graded in amplitude, and they may persist long enough to add, even if the stimuli are of sub-threshold level. The neuron thus *transduces* the environmental change into a bioelectric potential which in turn is transformed into a *code* of spike potentials. Since the individual spikes are all-or-none (i.e., all have the same amplitude), information cannot be coded through variation in amplitude. Coding, however, can be accomplished by modulation of the frequency. Thus patterns and bursts of varying frequency are used to transmit information in sensory systems. This important aspect will be discussed further in the chapter which follows.

The neuronal membrane plays a central role in both non-propagated and propagated excitations. It separates ions of opposite charge in such a manner that a potential is established between the interior and the exterior of the cell. Fortunately, these electrical changes are of measurable magnitude, and they constitute indicators of activity for the physiologist. Such electrical signs are routinely used as a sort of "window" into the inner workings of the nervous system.

Potentials are developed as a result of unequal distribution of ions. Several factors contribute to the imbalance, including unequal rates of diffusion and active transport (see Chapter 2). The ion distribution typical of a resting vertebrate nerve fiber is shown diagrammatically in Fig. 8-1. The inner surface of the cell membrane is negatively charged, the outer positively charged. The concentrations of sodium ions and chloride ions are greater outside the cell than inside, while that of potassium ions is greater inside. Several factors are responsible for this separation. K^+ and Cl^- are both acted upon by opposing forces, i.e.,

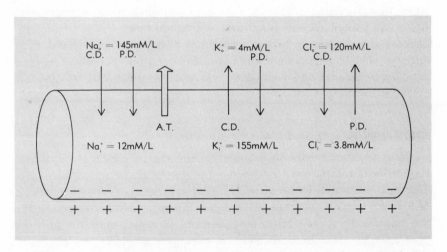

Fig. 8-1. The ionic distribution across the membrane of a typical mammalian nerve fibre. Concentrations are in millimoles per liter (1 millimole = 1/1000 mole). The arrows indicate the direction of the various forces acting on each ion, either active transport (A.T.), concentration differences (C. D.) or potential differences (P. D.). The unequal distribution generates a voltage across the membrane, negative on the inside and positive outside. When an impulse forms, sodium moves inward down its potential gradient and concentration gradient, momentarily reversing the polarity of the membrane (see text).

K^+ is drawn inward by the potential gradient and outward by its concentration gradient, while the Cl^- is drawn in by its concentration gradient but forced out of the cell by the potential gradient. The factors acting on Na^+ are both directed inward, but Na^+ is less diffusible in the resting membrane than is K^+. This is due, in part, to their relative sizes, hydrated Na^+ being about 5.12 A in diameter, while hydrated K^+ is about 3.96 A. It is thought that the pore size of the resting membrane is near the diameter of hydrated Na^+, which would account for the slowness of diffusion of Na^+ to the inside of the cell. The maintenance of a low sodium concentration inside the membrane, in spite of the inward forces, is however due mainly to a *sodium pump* which actively extrudes the ions against the gradients. It is presumed that the sodium pump is coupled at times to potassium movement in such a manner that for each sodium ion (or for several sodium ions) extruded, a potassium ion is moved inward. Clearly, such a coupled arrangement helps to minimize the potential which must be overcome in pumping the ions across the membrane. In spite of this, the energy demands of the sodium pump are sufficient to account for as much as one-third of the total energy expenditure of a resting nerve or muscle cell. It is believed that the actual charge separation is brought about by the rapid diffusion of K^+ ions outward, since this process is not accompanied by a like movement of negative charges. The resting membrane potential is therefore considered to be derived from the potassium potential. The resting potential which is actually developed and maintained amounts to about 0.07 to 0.09 volts (70-90 millivolts).

NERVE IMPULSE

Most neurons possess a segment of membrane which is capable of supporting an all-or-none electrical change, the nerve impulse or spike. The spike potential is produced by a large increase in the permeability of a small local area of the membrane. We must assume therefore that the impulse is accompanied by a change in membrane structure and pore size. The membrane becomes especially permeable to Na^+, which then flows into the cell in response to its concentration and potential gradients. Sodium continues to flow inward until the interior of the cell is positively charged (positive overshoot of Fig. 8-2B). At this point, sodium is again pumped out and K^+ moves in to return the membrane potential to the normal resting level (negative interior). Fig. 8-2A shows diagrammatically how a nerve impulse may be measured in an axon. The changes in potential which accompany the impulse are shown in

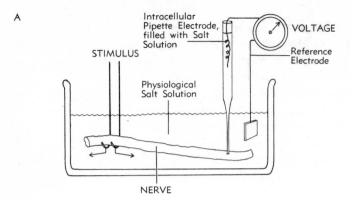

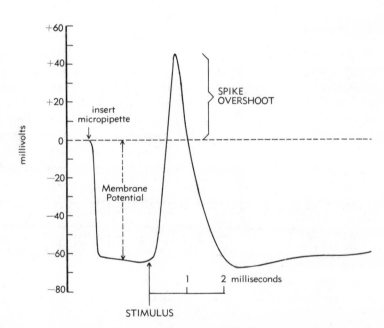

Fig. 8-2. (A) Procedure for stimulating and recording from a large axon. Following electrical stimulation an impulse spreads over the membrane in both directions. The pipette electrode inside the axon records the potential change across the membrane with respect to the reference electrode in the bathing solution. (B) The magnitude and time course of an action potential recorded as in (A). When the micropipette electrode is first inserted into the axon, a negative potential of about 70 millivolts is recorded. After stimulating the nerve electrically, an impulse or action potential is initiated which passes the pipette electrode giving a potential change. During the impulse, the negative membrane potential is abolished and the interior of the cell becomes momentarily positive before it returns again to the resting level. This entire process requires only about 1/500 of a second (2 milliseconds).

Fig. 8-2B. These electrical changes are propagated without decrement from one region of the cell to another distant region. Typically, the spike-supporting portion of the membrane is confined to the longer extensions of the cell, i.e., the axons. The nerve impulse, therefore, offers a means of communicating signals over long distances. Because of the necessity for rapid adjustments of muscles and equally demanding requirements for rapid processing of large amounts of sensory and stored information, the conduction velocity of the larger axons is often as high as 100 meters/second. The transmission of impulses to adjacent neurons occurs at synapses. The properties of these special membrane areas will be described in the next chapter.

PHOTORECEPTORS

Visual systems are both morphologically and physiologically complex. A single human retina is estimated to contain more than a hundred million receptor cells — the *rods* and *cones*. It is of interest to note that apparently both rods and cones have developed from the ciliated lining of the embryonic optic vesicle. Morphological evidence of this origin can be seen in the functional rod or cone as a modified cilium which holds the outer and inner segments of the rod or cone together. Retinas are multi-layered, showing at least two major synaptic regions, and perhaps a half dozen major morphological types of neuronal elements. As the neurons course toward the brain, many cross connections are made between adjacent elements (Fig. 8-3).

In vertebrate eyes, the light is directed to the retina by the cornea and lens. Although the cornea is the major refractive surface, the active focusing of light on the retina (accomodation) is achieved by changing the curvature of the lens.

In order to excite the receptors, light energy must first be absorbed. This is accomplished by the retinal pigments. All known visual pigments are composed of conjugated proteins containing vitamin A aldehyde, or retinaldehyde, as the chromophore (Fig. 8-4). These pigments are variously named rhodopsin, iodopsins, prophyropsins etc., depending upon the type of retinaldehyde and protein composing them. Apparently all of these pigments absorb light from the blue to the red wave length region between about 400 and 700 millimicrons (also called nanometers), with the highest absorption taking place in the green region near 500 millimicrons.

Light absorption has only *one* effect in the visual process, that is to convert retinaldehyde from isomer (11-*cis*) to another (all-*trans*)

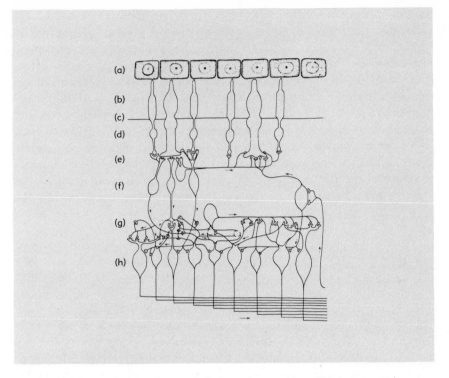

Fig. 8-3. Simplified diagram of the vertebrate retina. The innermost layer (a) in most animals contains a light-absorbing pigment which prevents light reflection back toward the receptor cells, the rods and cones (b) (c) (d). In nocturnal animals, however, layer (a) sometimes contains a reflecting pigment. The segments of the rods (thin elements) and cones (thick elements) labeled (b) contain the visual pigments. Second-order neurons (f) form numerous synaptic connections with both the receptors (e) and the ganglion cells at (g). Impulses are carried to the brain by the optic nerve which consists of the axons of the ganglion cells (h). Numerous lateral connections are provided which can excite or inhibit adjacent elements in the system. The arrows indicate some of the pathways for interaction of the various neurons. It is by this means that a code is transmitted to the brain. The path of light to the receptor elements traverses the other layers (from bottom of diagram to top). (From B. T. Scheer, **Animal Physiology,** John Wiley & Sons, Inc., New York, London, 1963.)

(Fig. 8-4, 5). The unstable configuration of 11-*cis* retinaldehyde allows a very efficient isomerization by light. The isomerization to the all-*trans* form probably influences the internal bonding of the protein opsin, since the latter undergoes some spontaneous changes following illumination (Fig. 8-5). These changes are thought to involve an unfolding of the

105

protein, since two sulfhydryls appear and one proton is released per molecule. The unfolding of the protein may well be a major event in excitation, since it could lead to the permeability changes in the membrane of the receptor element. In some receptors, metarhodopsin is reasonably stable, but in others, e.g., those of the vertebrates, the molecule cleaves into free opsin and retinaldehyde. Regeneration of the visual pigment requires an enzymatic isomerization of the retinaldehyde and an apparently spontaneous reformation of rhodopsin.

In some manner, yet to be clearly elucidated, these events lead to the formation of a generator potential in the receptor cells and impulse transmission in the ganglion cells (Fig. 8-3). The nervous pathway, as noted above, has numerous lateral interconnections, even within the

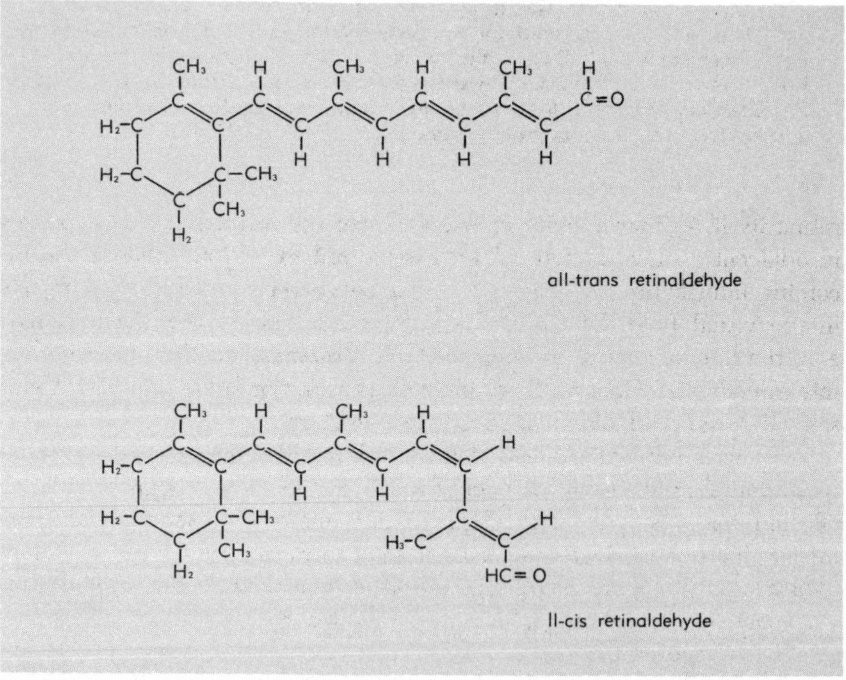

all-trans retinaldehyde

ll-cis retinaldehyde

Fig. 8-4. Representation of the two functional isomers of retinaldehyde compounds derived from half of a vitamin A molecule. The visual pigment rhodopsin is formed by the attachment of the aldehyde end (—CHO) of retinaldehyde to an amino group (NH_2) of opsin. The lower structure, 11-**cis** retinaldehyde is unstable. In the presence of visible light it undergoes an isomerization to all-**trans** retinaldehyde which initiates other changes in the attached opsin thus leading to excitation of the receptor membrane (see Fig. 8-5 and the text discussion).

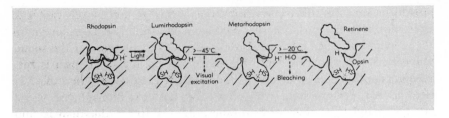

Fig. 8-5. The sequence of events following illumination of rhodopsin. At first, the 11-**cis** retinaldehyde is partially imbedded in the protein opsin. Light absorption isomerizes retinaldehyde from the 11-**cis** to the all-**trans** form (lumirhodopsin, second diagram). This introduces an instability into the protein opsin and it begins to unfold (metarhodopsin, third diagram). The reaction terminates in the cleavage of all-**trans** retinaldehyde from opsin (fourth diagram). The close association between rhodopsin and the membrane of the receptor cell allows this series of reactions to alter the permeability of the membrane to ions. As indicated in the second diagram, excitation may be triggered by the early events. It should be noted that light exerts only one effect in this sequence. It is responsible for the initial isomerization; the subsequent events are spontaneous. (From G. Wald and R. Hubbard, "Enzymatic Aspects of the Visual Processes," in: **The Enzymes,** 2nd edition, Vol. 3 B. Academic Press, Inc., New York, 1960.)

retina itself, so that activity in one receptor cell influences the responses in adjacent pathways. Lateral inhibition and excitation enhance the incoming information on shadows, edges, movements and forms of objects in the visual field. The brain centers which process the visual signals e.g., the *lateral geniculate nuclei* of the *thalamus* and the *visual cortex,* integrate the information from the retinal receptor fields into visual sensations of shape, movement, brightness and color.

The sensitivity of a dark-adapted rod is truly phenomenal. A single quantum of light (minimal energy unit) in the wave length range near 500 millimicrons (blue-green light) is adequate to excite one rod! This means that only a *single molecule* of rhodopsin has been affected. There is obviously some extremely high *amplification* of the basic photochemical event, since millions of ions move during the excitation process.

The eyes of arthropods and molluscs are morphologically different from those described for the vertebrates, although they are generally equally complex. Retinal pigments of the invertebrates, on the other hand, are very similar to the vertebrate compounds. A number of invertebrates possess, in addition to complex eyes, some relatively simple or even unicellular photoreceptive structures which seem to mediate a specific behavioral response. Certain clams, for example, have light-sensitive pallial nerves which reflexly cause siphon withdrawal in response to shadows. The anterior dermal layers of earthworms are also light sensitive. The radial nerves of several sea urchins have been shown to be photoreceptive and are presumed to mediate some of the spine movement reflexes. Perhaps the best known of these primitive photoreceptors is that found in the sixth abdominal ganglion of crayfish. Two neurons are present here which function not only as primary photoreceptors, but also as interneurons capable of being activated by the touch receptor hairs of the telson and uropods (tail appendages). The only known function of this receptor is that of initiating a locomotor response.

HEARING

Since auditory systems respond to airborne vibrations, the ear is a distance receptor, at least of intermediate range. Auditory information makes the animal aware of noises in his environment and provides a mechanism of communication; in certain animals, echo location constitutes the major means of orientation. The higher vertebrates and the insects possess the most sensitive and highly evolved auditory systems among animals, and as one might expect, these animals are also the ones capable of producing sounds.

In the auditory apparatus of mammals (Fig. 8-6), sound vibrations are first picked up by the tympanum, then transmitted by the middle ear bones into the oval window of the cochlea. The receptors, or *hair cells,* are located on an elastic partition within the cochlea known as the *basilar membrane.* Vibrations within the cochlea are transmitted inward to various distances, the distance being dependent on the frequency of the vibration. High frequency sounds, for example, move only a short column of fluid but are capable of displacing the short elastic strands of the proximal portion of the basilar membrane (Fig. 8-6). As a result, high frequency sounds stimulate the receptors close to the oval window. Low frequency vibrations, on the other hand, are capable of displacing a long column of fluid and of moving the distal portion of the basilar membrane. Frequency (pitch) discrimination is therefore determined in part by the site of vibration on the basilar membrane, while intensity (loudness) is determined in part by the amplitude of vibration. Finally, auditory signals are transmitted into the central nervous system along the auditory branch of the eighth cranial nerve.

The frequency range detectable by the average human lies between about 30 and 17,000 cycles per second (cycles per second are also called Hertz; Hz). The frequency range of hearing in other animals often extends considerably beyond this. In the region near 1700 cps, which is the peak sensitivity range for the human, a sound is audible if it displaces the tympanum only 1×10^{-5} to 1×10^{-9} centimeters! Absolute sensitivity of hearing in other animals probably does not exceed this, because if it did, the molecular vibrations in the auditory structures themselves would constitute an adequate stimulus.

Auditory functions are probably most specialized in those animals that utilize echo location. The insectivorous bats, for example, use their hearing as the major means of avoiding obstacles in flight and of locating prey. It has been shown by Donald Griffin of Rockefeller University, that hearing essentially replaces the sense of sight in these animals. They emit short sound pulses (about 2 milliseconds, or 1/500 second, in duration) of high frequency (40-90 kilocycles per second) and of high intens-

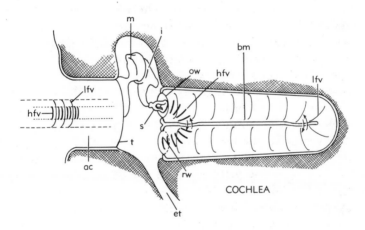

Fig. 8-6. A diagrammatic representation of the auditory portion of a mammalian ear. Sound vibrations of high frequency (h. f. v.) and of low frequency (l. f. v.) enter the auditory canal (a. c.) and induce vibration of the tympanum (t). These small movements are transmitted through the malleus (m), incus (i), and stapes (s) bones to the oval window (o. w.) of the fluid-filled cochlea. High frequency vibrations are transmitted through the fluid and across the proximal end of the basilar membrane (b. m.) while low frequency vibrations cross the basilar membrane near the distal end. The basilar membrane contains the vibration receptors (hair cells) which are stimulated as a result of displacement. The vibrations are then dissipated as they leave the round window (r. w.) and enter the eustachian tube (e. t.). The cochlea, represented here as a straight tube, is actually coiled in most mammals.

ity from their vocal cords. After being reflected by objects in the environment, these sounds return as echoes that are interpreted to give the bat data on the size, distance, direction and rate of movement of the reflecting object. Short duration pulses are needed for effective echoes, since the pulse must not extend in space more than twice the distance to the reflecting object. Sound in air travels 344 meters per second; a one millisecond (1/1000 sec) pulse therefore extends 34.4 cm; a 2 msec pulse about 70 cm. This is an important factor if the bat is to be able to get close enough to capture insects in flight. High frequency (i.e., short wave length) sound is required for reflecting off a small object such as a mosquito. If the wave length of the sound is appreciably longer than the diameter of the reflecting object, the echo is smeared with consequent loss of intensity and direction. Finally, intense cries are needed since energy is lost in the course of transmission both to and from the reflecting object as well as by direct absorption at the object's surface.

Bats have a remarkable ability to detect their own echoes in the midst of noise of similar frequency and intensity. For example, if several bats are confined to a small dark room, each can catch insects in flight and at the same time avoid one another as well as extraneous foreign objects. This is accomplished in spite of the fact that each individual is continually emitting similar cries which are potentially capable of "jamming" the sonar of their fellows.

As is well known, porpoises also utilize echo location in orientation and food capture. Although the mechanisms used by porpoises are similar to those described for bats, the necessity of using short pulses is even more critical for them, since sound travels much faster in water (1550 meters/sec) than in air.

CHEMORECEPTION

Some sensitivity to the chemical make-up of the environment appears to be universal. The receptors may respond to chemicals carried in air or water, or they may require direct contact. A blowfly or a butterfly can taste with the feet as well as the mouth parts, while crustaceans generally have chemoreceptors scattered on the antennules, mouth parts, legs and gill chambers. Sedentary animals such as clams or tubiculous worms, taste the environment by means of receptors located in the ventilation stream. There seem to be no particular morphological features which distinguish chemoreceptors from other peripheral sensory neurons, although in most organisms the chemoreceptor cells are usually small. Common to all chemoreceptors is the property of producing generator potentials as a result of contact with a wide spectrum of chemicals, often in quite low concentrations. The details of this process are almost totally unknown. It is speculated that the specific sites on receptor membranes are capable of interacting with various classes of molecules, according to their overall stereochemical form. Presumably, when a fit is made be- tweeen the stimulating molecule and the membrane, an excitation is somehow generated in the receptor cell.

There are many interesting examples of the use of chemical senses in orientation and species recognition. An excellent example of this is the work of V. Twitty of Stanford. If the newt, *Taricha rivularis,* is displaced several miles from its home stream, it will travel overland and even across foreign streams to return. If blinded, it is still capable of homing, which indicates that celestial and topographical navigation are of little importance. If the olfactory tract is severed, however, the ability to home is almost totally lost. When large numbers of tagged animals are dis- placed, most will return home immediately, or at the first breeding sea- son. Others may not return for several years, but eventually as many as 90% may be recaptured in their home stream. This is indicative of a memory or "imprinting" of chemical information characteristic of the home stream. A similar homing behavior is exhibited by salmon. After hatching in freshwater streams, the young salmon navigate down-river to the ocean where they grow to maturity. Several years later the sexually mature animals navigate, probably by using celestial cues, to the mouth of their home river system. They then swim upstream avoiding foreign tributaries, and with surprising accuracy they eventually locate the stream in which they hatched several years previously.

Many insects are known to respond to species- and sex-specific chemi- cals which mediate a fixed behavior pattern. These compounds, called *pheromones,* generally trigger a complex response similar to that obtained from a hormone, but pheromones differ from the latter in being trans- ported by air or substrate rather than through the blood. In addition, they are released from special exocrine structures on the body surface rather than originating from the endocrine structures typical of hor- mones. The simplest acting pheromones seem to "release" an instinctive and stereotyped behavior pattern. Others appear first to stimulate the central nervous system which in turn "primes" an endocrine system to induce the final effect. Pheromones are employed extensively by colonial insects to mark food sources or trails and also as alarm substances. Non- colonial as well as colonial species utilize these substances as sex attract- ants. The miniscule concentration of attractant to which a male of the species will respond is astounding — probably no more is required than a few hundred molecules per cubic centimeter! The crossing of scent trails of two species does not create confusion because the chemicals, the receptors, and the evoked behavior patterns are all species specific.

Finally we should mention the existence of several important internal chemical-sensing systems, such as the O_2-sensitive structures associated with the carotid arteries, the CO_2-sensitive receptors of the respiratory center of the medulla and the osmoreceptors of the hypothalamus. These sensory centers operate as parts of control systems that maintain the chemical composition of the internal environment within the range consistent with life processes.

THE SENSATIONS OF POSITION, TOUCH, PAIN AND TEMPERATURE

A number of receptors are associated with the muscles, tendons and joints. These are collectively called proprioceptors. Basically, they are mechanoreceptors which respond to distortions of their special terminals. The proprioceptors translate relatively large movements of the body into bioelectric signals. The signals, in turn, inform the central nervous system of position, as well as the rate and magnitude of movements of the various parts of the body. One type of proprioceptor, the *muscle spindle*, is derived from highly specialized skeletal muscle fibers. The receptor consists of a stretch-sensitive nerve terminal coiled around the central part of the specialized muscle. A stretch or pull applied to the muscle bundle distorts the terminals and excites the sensory neuron. Stretch-sensitive terminals of a different kind are also found on the tendons of most skeletal muscles. These receptors, called *Golgi tendon organs*, signal mainly the load that is supported by the muscle. Proprioceptive signals generally do not reach the conscious level directly, but are sent instead to the cerebellum where they are incorporated into the muscle adjustment responses. The vestibular apparatus of the inner ear contributes additional information concerning the direction of gravity and linear acceleration (macula of the utricle). Information on angular acceleration of the body is obtained from receptors in the semicircular canals. The latter information is of value to the brain in making appropriate muscle adjustments for the overall motor functions such as equilibrium maintenance and walking. Pressure changes throughout all the tissues are sensed by the specialized *Pacinian corpuscles* and by numerous free nerve endings which respond to distortion of the surrounding tissues. These may adapt rather rapidly, so these receptors are of most value in detecting transient changes.

The body surface is densely supplied with touch, pain and temperature-sensitive terminals, but most of the sensory information obtained from the visceral regions is in the form of diffuse pain. In contrast to the proprioceptive senses, all of these reach the conscious level.

WEAK ELECTRIC FISH AND A NEW CLASS OF RECEPTORS

In addition to the powerful electric fishes described in the previous chapter, several families of freshwater fishes, particularly the Gymnotidae (knife fish of South America), the Mormyridae (elephant-trunk fishes of Africa) and *Gymnarchus niloticus* are known as weak electric fish because of their ability to produce repetitive low voltage pulses (Fig. 8-7). Most of these are small hardy animals that live so well in home aquariums that they are now sold commercially (Fig. 8-8). If the opportunity arises you may wish to observe their interesting locomotion and behavior.

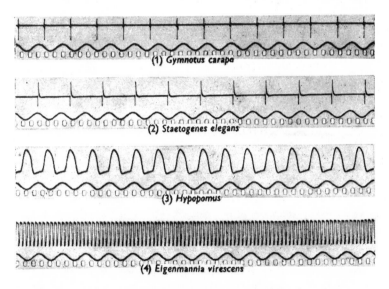

(1) Gymnotus carapo

(2) Staetogenes elegans

(3) Hypopomus

(4) Eigenmannia virescens

Fig. 8-7. Typical low voltage pulses produced by four gymnotid knife fish. The pulses of **Gymnotus carapo** (1) and **Staetogenes elegans** (2) are diphasic and extremely brief, while those of **Hypopomus** (3) are more prolonged and monophasic. **Eigenmannia** (4) produces high frequency pulses of intermediate duration. Time signal, 50 cycles per second; temperature 25°C. The amplitude is approximately 0.5-1.0 volts at the body surface in most weak electric fish. (From W. H. Lissmann, **J. Exptl. Biol.,** 35: 156, 1958.)

It has long been assumed that the powerful electric fishes use their capability as a weapon. Only recently, however, has the function of the harmless discharge of the weak electric fish been explained, i.e., as part of an "electrical guidance" system. The discovery of this function led to the disclosure of a new class of receptors — the electroreceptors.

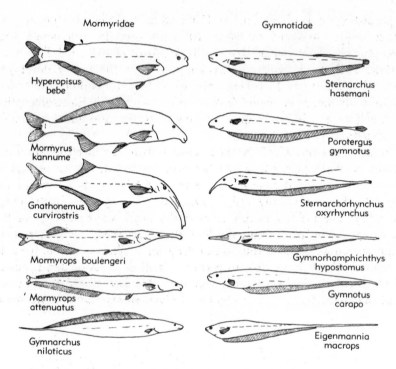

Fig. 8-8. The characteristic body forms of weak electric fish. Note the elongated fins and "naked tails" of the Gymnotidae and of **Gymnarchus niloticus** (Gymarchidae). (From H. W. Lissmann, **J. Exptl. Biol.**, 35: 156, 1958.)

In weak electric fish, the organization of the electroplaques and the behavior of their membranes is generally similar to those of the powerful electric fish. The most interesting aspect of the electrical discharge from these animals is its continuous and often rhythmical nature. Certain of the gymnotids discharge at relatively low frequencies (*Gymnotus carapo*, 50/sec) which are modifiable by various sensory inputs, including tapping on the aquarium, feeding, and periods of activity. In others, the frequency is high (*Eigenmannia virescens*, 300/sec) and apparently unmodified by the sensory input (Fig. 8-7). It is interesting to note that discharges from certain of the gymnotids have been recorded at frequencies as high as 1600/sec! One should remember that the pulses from these high frequency fish are incessant. If an animal produces 1000 pulses per second, this amounts to 60,000/minute and 86.4 million per day!

According to H. Lissmann of Cambridge, the high frequency, low voltage pulses produced by these fishes are used in conjunction with a receptor system of remarkable sensitivity. Most of these fish have poor eyesight and do not, as far as we know, possess the highly developed chemical senses typical, for example, of catfish. In addition, they live in murky streams and ponds and are often nocturnal. Electroreception has therefore evolved as a major means of orientation and localization of objects and prey.

In most, but not all of the weak electric fish, the electroplaques are oriented so that at discharge, the tail becomes negative with respect to the head. The current flow follows a path of low resistance out of the body into the surrounding water (Fig. 8-9). The specific electroreceptors, which are located mainly around the head region and along the side of the body, have unusually low electrical resistance with respect to the surrounding skin, thus completing an electrical circuit back to the animal. The fish are able to perceive small changes or distortions in the electrical field around them and turn this into useful information about the environment. The receptors of *Gymnarchus niloticus* are sensi-

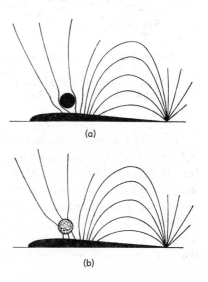

Fig. 8-9. The dipole-like nature of the electric field surrounding the weak electric fish **Gymnarchus niloticus.** (a) Distortion of the field as a result of the presence of an object of low conductivity. (b) Modification of the field due to an object of high conductivity. The electrical receptors are used to interpret these distortions and thus gain information about the environment. (From H. W. Lissmann and K. E. Machin. **Jour. Exptl. Biol.** 35: 451, 1958.)

(a)

(b)

tive to minute electrical gradients of the order of a few microvolts/centimeter. Major changes in the electrical field are produced by objects of high conductivity (e.g. metals) and also by insulators (e.g. glass) in the environment (Fig. 8-9). With sensitivities perhaps in excess of those measurable by human experimental techniques, the animals are capable of readily detecting the differences between stones, logs, leaves or other fish in their vicinity. The receptors are thought to code their signals primarily by a change in response frequency that is proportional to the magnitude of the electrical pulse received, i.e., by a "pulse frequency modulation." According to this scheme, strong signals, derived from the presence of conductors in the electric field, would produce higher frequencies of discharge in receptor neurons than would attenuated pulses resulting from the presence of an insulator. Phase coding (perhaps this actually involves latency coding) has also been shown to occur in receptor units of certain gymnotids. By this term, it is meant that the time relationship between the spikes evoked in the receptors and the electrical pulses themselves is modified by the presence of objects in the fish's environment.

It is of interest to note that all the weak electric fish have developed either an elongated dorsal fin (*Gymnarchus* and several mormyrids) or an extensive anal fin (most gymnotids). This adaptation allows the animals to hold their bodies straight, but at the same time to propel themselves through the water by undulations of the major fin (Fig. 8-8). It is fascinating to observe swimming in these fish; they seem to glide effortlessly in either a forward or backward direction without moving the body. This is apparently more than an esthetic factor; the body must be held in a rigid position to insure that the surrounding electrical field retains a constant relationship between the position of the pulse-emitting (tail) and pulse-receiving (head) loci.

Interesting morphological changes are apparent in the brains of the weak electric fish, when compared to their non-electric relatives. Typically, there is an enormous expansion in the region of the cerebellum, which is thought to comprise the integration or computation center responsible for interpreting the electrical signals.

REFERENCES

BULLOCK, T. H., and HORRIDGE, G. A., *Structure and Function in Nervous Systems of Invertebrates*, San Francisco: W. H. Freeman and Co., 1965. Vol. I and II.

CARTHY, J. D., *An Introduction to the Behavior of Invertebrates*. London: Allen and Unwin, 1958.

CHAGAS, CAROLOS, and PAES DE CARVALHO, ANTONIO, (eds.), *Bioelectrogenesis,* Amsterdam: Elsevier Pub. Co., 1961.

GRIFFIN, D. R., *Listening in the Dark,* New Haven: Yale University Press, 1958.

GRUNDFEST, H., "Electric Fishes." *Scientific American,* October, 1960, p. 115.

LISSMANN, H. W. "Electric Location by Fishes." *Scientific American,* March, 1963, p. 50.

PROSSER, C. L., and BROWN, F. A., JR., *Comparative Animal Physiology,* 2nd ed. Philadelphia: W. B. Saunders Co., 1961. Ch. 10, 11, 12.

RAMSAY, J. A., *A Physiological Approach to the Lower Animals,* Cambridge University Press, 1952. Ch. 6.

ROEDER, KENNETH D., *Nerve Cells and Insect Behavior,* Cambridge, Massachusetts: Harvard University Press, 1963.

CHAPTER 9

Nervous
systems

INTRODUCTION

Nervous systems of higher animals are made up of millions of cells, each of which is capable of producing hundreds of impulses (action potentials) per second. Clearly, if only a fraction of these cells were active at any one time, the coded information they could convey would be astounding. We find, in fact, that many of the cells are active simultaneously. As a result, an enormous mass of diverse information must be processed continually and then directed either to storage or to appropriate effector systems. The information upon which the integrative operations are performed originates primarily from the receptors, but some is derived from spontaneously active cells within the central nervous system.

Nervous systems have been studied at various levels of organization and function, beginning with the physiology of single neurons. Since information is transmitted from unit to unit in any nervous system, and since codes are involved in this process, many workers have concentrated their efforts on the problems of cellular communication and information coding. Any comprehensive study of nervous systems also tries to account for the complex behavior of the animal in terms of the underlying processes.

The brief treatment of nervous integration which follows includes the results of studies made at each of these levels. The examples are taken from mammalian nervous systems because it is felt that their structure and function will be most familiar, and that this advantage will outweigh the disadvantages arising from their complexity.

SYNAPTIC TRANSMISSION

Communication between neurons is accomplished at specific sites where adjacent cells come close together. These sites, the synapses, essentially assume the role of one-way valves that direct information from one part of the system to another. Knowledge of the existence of these important structures dates back only to the turn of the present century when Ramon y Cajal observed that neurons were indeed separate from one another. Sir Charles Scott Sherrington, who named the structures, went on to make major contributions to our understanding of reflex function in the nervous system by characterizing the actions of neurons which were synaptically associated.

Synapses are now known to be made up of two specialized portions of neuronal membrane. One membrane area is located on the axon terminals of the presynaptic cell, and the other is found on the cell body of the postsynaptic cell (Fig. 9-1). The two interacting neurons are separated from one another by a small distance of only about 100 to 500 Angstroms which is called the synaptic cleft. The dimensions of this tiny but important space as well as some of the morphological details of the two synaptic surfaces have been revealed by the use of electron microscopy.

Transmission of excitation across this synaptic cleft is dependent upon the release of a "transmitter" substance from the presynaptic terminal which then diffuses to the postsynaptic surface where is produces

Fig. 9-1. A diagram of a synapse showing its most important structural components. The presynaptic neuron terminates in an expanded structure that is separated from the postsynaptic cell by a narrow synaptic cleft. Transmitter, contained in the synaptic vesicles, is released from the presynaptic terminal by impulses arriving over the axon. After diffusing across the synaptic cleft, the transmitter alters the permeability of the subsynaptic membrane to ions. As described in the text, this permeability change can lead to an excitation or inhibition of the postsynaptic cell. (From E. Florey, "Recent Studies on Synaptic Transmitters," **American Zoologist** 2: 45-54, 1962.)

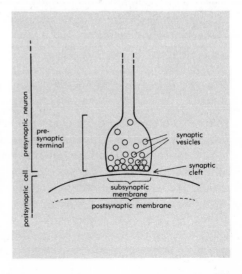

an effect (Fig. 9-2). The response may be either an excitation or an inhibition of the postsynaptic cell.

In a resting nerve cell the potential across the outside membrane is about 75 millivolts. The transmitter presumably acts by changing the permeability of the postsynaptic membrane and thereby the membrane potential. For example, a small increase in general permeability to several ions reduces the potential of the postsynaptic cell about 15-20 milli-

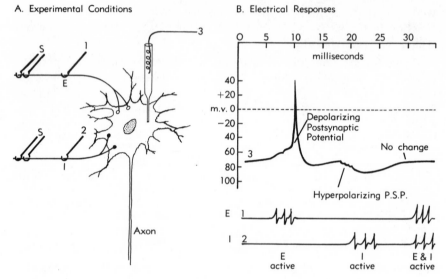

Fig. 9-2. Intracellular potential changes of a postsynaptic neuron in response to excitatory synaptic inputs (E) (depolarizing), inhibitory synaptic inputs (I) (hyperpolarizing) and a simultaneous E and I effect (neutralized). The experimental arrangement is presented in (A). The records obtained from the extracellular electrodes of the presynaptic cells (1 and 2) are shown in (B), along with the record from the intracellular electrode (3) in the postsynaptic cell. m.v.-millivolts; P. S. P.-postsynaptic potential.

volts, at which point there is a rapid sodium influx which gives rise to a propagated impulse. This constitutes a depolarizing or excitatory response to the transmitter. The reaction between the postsynaptic neuronal membrane and the transmitter can also result in an inhibition, or hyperpolarization. Hyperpolarization, derived from an increase in K^+ and Cl^- permeability, blocks the effects of excitatory postsynaptic depolarization.

Not all of the transmitter substances operating in nervous systems are known. Acetylcholine has been established as the transmitter for the myoneural junction, for some of the cells of the autonomic nervous system and for certain cells of the central nervous system. Norepinephrine is also known to be involved in synaptic transmission in some of the autonomic cells and is perhaps involved in other parts of the nervous system as well. Other compounds, including gamma-aminobutyric acid and 5-hydroxytryptamine (serotonin) have been implicated as transmitters, but their participation is not definitely established. The characteristics which determine whether an effect is excitatory or inhibitory probably reside in the type of transmitter released and in the nature of the synaptic membrane of the postsynaptic cell. Acetylcholine, for example, may produce an excitatory reaction in some parts of the nervous system and an inhibitory effect in others.

Some valuable information on synaptic transmission has been obtained from studies using special drugs which interfere in some way with normal transmitter function. For example, a drug might bind itself to the receptor sites of the postsynaptic membrane so firmly that the transmitter cannot reach them. Other compounds act as inhibitors of the enzymes which destroy the transmitter. In the presence of this second type of drug, the transmitter persists and its effect on the postsynaptic cell is increased. Finally, there are numerous drugs which in one way or another mimic the effects of natural transmitters giving either an inhibition or an excitation. One can see therefore that careful use of such compounds allows the experimenter selectively to activate or inactivate certain parts of the nervous system and observe the behavioral or physiological response. Recently, drugs have been applied by micropipette directly on or into individual neurons to facilitate even more detailed studies of synaptic transmission.

The postsynaptic cell often requires a burst of incoming action potentials (multiple doses of transmitter) before it responds to the extent of spiking. The postsynaptic potentials apparently decay slowly enough to allow several incoming impulses to add algebraically, a process called summation (Fig. 9-3). It is important to realize therefore that synaptic transmission does not give rise to an all-or-none response directly each time an impulse arrives from the presynaptic cell. Instead, a graded series of events can occur that may range from complete excitation to complete inhibition, depending upon the time sequence of impulse arrival and the kinds of transmitters that are being released.

CODING OF INFORMATION

Information is transmitted through the long processes of the nerve cells by arranging the impulses in the form of codes. In a way, this is

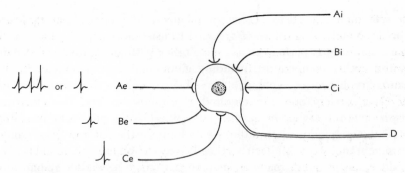

Fig. 9-3. Summation. Assume three excitatory impulses are needed to fire cell (D) above. They may arrive appropriately spaced as a burst from A_e alone, or as three separate impulses arriving in a properly timed sequence from A_e, B_e and C_e. Cell (D) may be inhibited completely or the threshold may be heightened by impulses arriving from inhibitory neurons A_i, B_i and C_i.

similar to Morse code, except nerves do not use dots and dashes, but only impulses or spikes. Since each cell produces action potentials of only one size, the code cannot take the form of a series of impulses of different amplitude. But a nerve cell is capable of carrying information by assuming different patterns of discharge (Fig. 9-4). Note that all of the patterns shown in Fig. 9-4 are identical in the total number of spikes

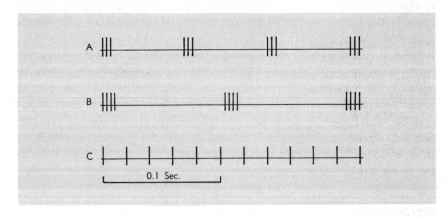

Fig. 9-4. Diagram of a hypothetical code of information being transferred along an axon. Three patterns of impulses are shown, all at the same average frequency. Each of these patterns produce a different effect on the postsynaptic cell thereby conveying different information (see text). If the activity varies both in overall frequency and in pattern of discharge, an even greater amount of information can be transmitted.

per unit time (i.e., the average frequency is the same), but they are capable of conveying quite different information to the postsynaptic cell. Again, consider the synapse as capable of algebraic addition of the incoming events. Also, recall that time is an important parameter in the accumulating process. If the spikes arrive in rapid succession, they are added effectively because transmitter accumulates and the electrical properties of the membrane are favorable. Using our example (Fig. 9-4A) we might expect an addition of events such that one spike would occur in the postsynaptic cell for every three incoming spikes. If the impulses come in quadruplets as in (B) they may be added much more effectively and give two spikes in the postsynaptic cell for four incoming ones. An evenly spaced pattern such as (C) may result in only one postsynaptic impulse for eight incoming ones, since there may be some decay of excitation between incoming spikes. In effect, a considerable amount of information can be coded and passed from one cell to the next merely by arranging the temporal pattern of arriving impulses, even if we confine our example to one frequency. If the frequency as well as the pattern is altered, the coding possibilities become almost limitless. In addition, a presynaptic cell does not have to produce a spike in the postsynaptic cell to convey information. If the presynaptic cell only prepares the adjacent cell to fire or inhibits it to a slight degree, it nevertheless has had an effect.

The remaining sections of this chapter contain a brief presentation of the major pathways of information transmission in a complex nervous system. The motor system is introduced first since it shows most clearly how multiple synaptic transmission contributes directly to behavior. This is followed by a look at sensory transmission which exemplifies the importance of neuronal circuitry in directing the other parts of the nervous system. The remaining discussion on the brain is offered to convey two general ideas. First, we will see how the sensory and memory information is refined and interpreted before it flows out to the muscles and glands. Second, we will consider the interactions of various parts of the brain in relation to other functions of the nervous system that are not directly related to the activation of effectors.

MOTOR SYSTEM

In mammalian brains, a specific area of the cerebrum assumes control of the voluntary musculature. If this *motor cortex* is stimulated electrically, a specific group of muscles in the periphery will contract (Fig. 9-5). Exploration of the brain surface with the stimulating electrodes

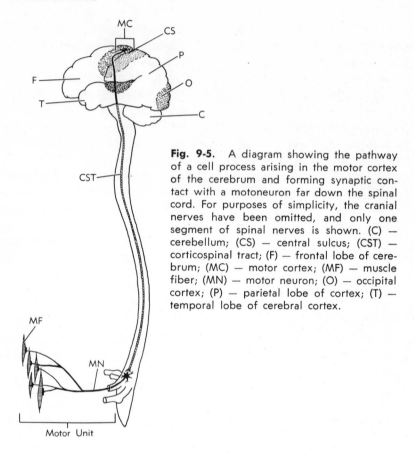

Fig. 9-5. A diagram showing the pathway of a cell process arising in the motor cortex of the cerebrum and forming synaptic contact with a motoneuron far down the spinal cord. For purposes of simplicity, the cranial nerves have been omitted, and only one segment of spinal nerves is shown. (C) — cerebellum; (CS) — central sulcus; (CST) — corticospinal tract; (F) — frontal lobe of cerebrum; (MC) — motor cortex; (MF) — muscle fiber; (MN) — motor neuron; (O) — occipital cortex; (P) — parietal lobe of cortex; (T) — temporal lobe of cerebral cortex.

allows one to "map" the extent of the motor areas. Histological and electrophysiological examinations of the central nervous system show cell bodies in the cortex which send axons from the motor area down to the motoneuron cell bodies in the ventral gray matter of the spinal cord (Fig. 9-5). These axons follow specific motor tracts which are localized in the white matter. Each motoneuron (and thus each motor unit) is influenced by many synaptic inputs other than the axons from cells of the motor cortex. This multiple synaptic control is shown in Fig. 9-6. Since the motoneuron algebraically sums the various inputs it receives, it was aptly named "the final common path." If the excitatory impulses prevail, the motoneuron fires and each muscle fiber of that motor unit contracts. The motor cortex may be thought of as a prime mover, but sensory and proprioceptive information is also involved in making the decision. Complex motor function, such as balance or walking, involves continual processing of sensory information from such sources as the retina of the eye, the vestibular apparatus of the inner ear, and the stretch receptors of muscles, tendons and joints.

In some cases, local receptors may exert a rather direct effect on motoneuron function at the level of the spinal cord. One such case is the knee-jerk reflex which is induced by rapid stretch of the patellar tendons of the quadriceps muscles of the leg. Here, the signals which arise from the muscle spindles return directly to the motoneurons controlling the quadriceps muscles, causing these neurons to fire. This in turn results in a contraction of the quadriceps muscles, which opposes the force of the initial stretch. It is important to note that localized spinal reflexes of this type are not always apparent, since the local sensory effects can be almost completely overshadowed by the excitatory or inhibitory impulses that arise from higher centers. In fact, spinal transection often *enhances* the local reflex signs, since the excitatory or inhibitory signals from the brain are then unable to exert their modifying effects.

SENSORY TRANSMISSION

In addition to direct effects upon motor processes at the level of the spinal cord, somatic sensory information is also transmitted to the higher centers of the central nervous system. The axons of primary or secondary sensory neurons form prominent bundles which ascend the spinal

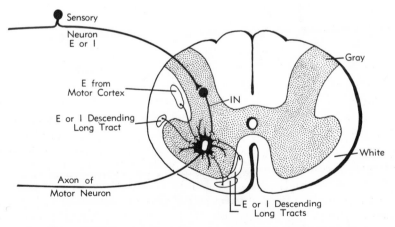

Fig. 9-6. Multiple synaptic inputs to a motor neuron showing the convergence of several excitatory (E) and inhibitory (I) long tracts descending from the brain and other parts of the spinal cord. The input from a local sensory neuron is interrupted by one of the numerous interneurons (IN) present in the spinal cord.

cord. There are two major pathways that sensory signals follow into the central nervous system. Proprioceptive signals generally are processed by the brain and then returned to the motoneuron output of the spinal cord without reaching the conscious level. Other sensory information is generally brought more immediately to the consciousness in the form of the familiar sensations of touch, pain, temperature and pressure. These signals follow a different course from those arising from proprioceptors. In general the tracts carrying conscious sensations ascend the spinal cord and synapse in the thalamus. From here, they project directly to the sensory cortex of the cerebrum (Fig. 9-7). In fact, all the incoming sensory tracts pass into the thalamus except those from the nasal epithelium and those which carry strictly proprioceptive data. The proprioceptive signals are processed by the cerebellum, the upper brain stem nuclei and the basal ganglia as well as the cerebral cortex. There exist, in essence, long circuit reflexes which begin with proprioceptive signals in

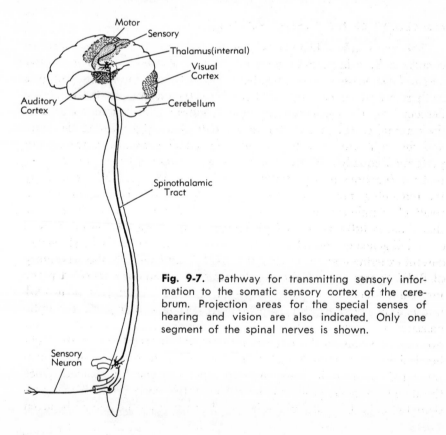

Fig. 9-7. Pathway for transmitting sensory information to the somatic sensory cortex of the cerebrum. Projection areas for the special senses of hearing and vision are also indicated. Only one segment of the spinal nerves is shown.

the periphery and ultimately involve hundreds or thousands of neurons in all levels of the central nervous system. This distribution of sensory information within the nervous system is understandable in light of the evolutionary development of higher vertebrate brains. The cerebellum evolved as a center which processed spinal sensory and vestibular signals prior to the appearance of the highly structured cerebral cortex. The olfactory input, on the other hand, was originally associated with a primitive cerebral layer which has long since been displaced by the present "new" cerebral cortex. Many of the functions performed by the new cerebral cortex of mammals are accomplished by the tectum (midbrain roof) and tegmentum (lateral walls and floor of the midbrain) in the birds, reptiles, amphibians and fishes. Although the cerebellum continued to expand in importance in the birds and mammals, the functions of the tectum have largely been assumed by the new cerebral cortex, particularly in the mammals.

ASSOCIATION OF THE CEREBRAL HEMISPHERES

The two cerebral hemispheres of the brains of higher mammals are connected by a large mass of fibers called the *corpus callosum,* or the *cerebral commissure.* There are therefore really "two brains" present, just as there are two ears, eyes, etc. Because of the crossing of fibers in their descent from the motor centers of the cerebrum, the left motor area of the cerebral cortex controls the movements of the right side of the body and the right area directs the left side. Other activities, however, are performed equally well by either hemisphere, as evidenced by the fact that the functions of a partially ablated hemisphere can be assumed by the remaining intact one. The corpus callosum may be sectioned by a relatively simple surgical procedure. Gross observations show, in general, that there is little superficial difference between the responses or even the intelligence of normal and splitbrain experimental animals. However, careful experimentation by several workers, particularly in the laboratory of R. W. Sperry at the California Institute of Technology, revealed many important functions of the commissure, as well as supplying additional information about cerebral function. In certain experiments, the optic chiasma was severed along with the corpus callosum so that the left eye reported only to the left hemisphere and the right eye to the right hemisphere. The animals were then trained to solve a certain problem presented to the right eye while the other eye was blindfolded. Once the animal became proficient in the task, the same problem was presented to only the "untrained left eye." In such cases the animal behaved as if it had never seen the problem before. A normal animal, of course, could have solved the problem with either eye regardless of which eye had been trained. To illustrate further the independence of the hemispheres, splitbrain animals lacking the optic chiasma have been trained to obtain opposite solutions to visual problems presented to each eye separately! The commissure then functions to transfer information from one hemisphere to the other. It has been shown that in such laboratory animals as cats, the information transfer occurs at the time it is received by the brain. In man, where one hemisphere is dominant, single engrams, or memory traces, are laid down in the dominant hemisphere only during the immediate learning process; however, this information may be transferred to the opposite hemisphere when required for the solution of a problem at some later date. Although the two halves of the cerebrum can perform many tasks alone, the associations provided by the commissure greatly increase the overall efficiency, particularly in the performance of tasks where both halves of the body are involved. For example, the commissures transfer the appropriate sensory data needed for coordination of opposing limbs as they are supplied by the paired eyes, ears, and vestibular organs, as well as from touch and pressure receptors located on opposite sides of the body.

OVERALL MOTOR COORDINATION OF RAPID MOVEMENTS

The execution of smooth, coordinated skeletal movements depends upon multiple interactions of many parts of the central nervous system, each contributing its own "processed" sensory, memory or command signals. Consider for example, the control of rapid limb movements as depicted diagrammatically in Fig. 9-8. Here, the *command* for movement arises in the voluntary motor cortex of the cerebrum. A *duplicate* of the command is sent to the cerebellum. The resulting movement generates sensory signals from the muscles, joints and tendons. Related visual cues and vestibular signals from the eyes and semicircular canals are also directed to the cerebellum. This sensory information measures the extent of the movement and, therefore, the *results* of the initial command. The cerebellum is thought to be able to *compare* the results of the command with the command itself. If there is an *error*, impulses are then sent to the appropriate muscles for correcting the movement. If there is an overshoot, for example, correcting excitatory impulses might be sent to the opposing muscles while inhibitory impulses are directed to the muscles which were initially activated by the command.

THE HYPOTHALAMUS AND AUTONOMIC NERVOUS SYSTEM

Localized lesions or stimulation in the region of the hypothalamus may result in marked changes in body temperature, osmotic balance, blood pressure, food intake, gastric secretion and even in some endocrine functions, particularly those of the pituitary. Most of these changes

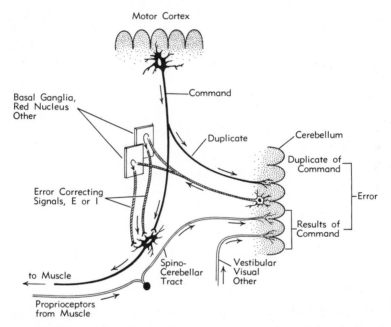

Fig. 9-8. A highly diagrammatic representation of the possible interactions between command and sensory signals in the control of muscular movements.

are regulatory in nature and are known to be adjusted by appropriate impulses in the autonomic nervous system (Fig. 9-9). The hypothalamus might properly be considered then as the major control center for a large number of autonomic functions.

The physiological events involved in the regulation of body temperature typify the control mechanisms performed by the hypothalamus (see Chapter 6). They include such autonomic controls as blood vessel diameter, sweating and pilorection. The relationships between the hypothalamus and endocrine regulation will be discussed in the last chapter.

The autonomic nervous system, therefore, operates in numerous reflex activities that are comparable to those performed by the somatic nervous

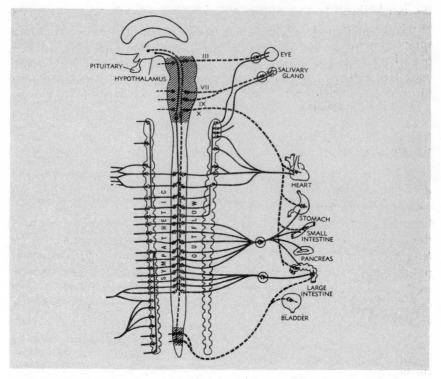

Fig. 9-9. The major features of the organization of the autonomic nervous system. Parasympathetic outflow arises from the brain stem and from the sacral cord (shaded) while sympathetic outflow occurs from the mid-portion of the cord. The numerals III, VII, IX and X refer to the cranial nerves having parasympathetic nerves within them. Sympathetic nerves are represented by solid lines while parasympathetic nerves are dashed. The two ganglionated chains on either side of the spinal cord belong to the sympathetic system. Examples of some of the major structures innervated by the autonomic system are shown at the extreme right. Nerves leaving the left side are distributed to the blood vessels, sweat glands and the piloerector muscles of hair. Only a few of the numerous connections between the hypothalamus and related brain structures are shown. Note that the outflow from both segments of the autonomic nervous system involves two neurons. Those leaving the central nervous system are called preganglionic, while those arising from peripheral ganglia are referred to as postganglionic. (From E. Gardner, **Fundamentals of Neurology,** 4th edition. W. B. Saunders, Phila. and London, 1963.)

system. Additional examples include such processes as defecation and urination. Sensory signals derived from the filling of the bowel or bladder initiate autonomic motor signals and reflex emptying. Autonomic activities are not under voluntary control; i.e., one cannot consciously control the rate of heart beat, the diameter of the pupil of the eye, or the size of blood vessels. The voluntary contraction and relaxation of striated sphincter muscles, however, does provide a means of conscious control of such reflexes as defecation and urination. It should be noted that spinal cord transection alters autonomic reflexes by eliminating the higher sources of excitation and inhibition in a manner comparable to that described for somatic reflexes.

THE INTERPRETIVE CORTEX

Association and integration of sensory and memory information is undoubtedly performed by many parts of the brain. One of the most interesting and thoroughly documented examples of this complex brain function has been described by a group of Canadian neurologists under the guidance of W. Penfield. Electrical stimulation of the surface of the *temporal lobes* (Fig. 9-5) of conscious human patients has been shown to produce two categories of response; the "experiential" and the "interpretive." In some cases the patient recalls in great detail the sights and sounds of some otherwise forgotten experience. These "experiential responses" occur at the onset of stimulation and disappear abruptly when stimulation ceases. The responses may be repeatedly brought forth by reapplying the electrodes to the same area of the brain. The experiences furthermore have been known to involve music, scenery or conversation that occurred many years past.

Stimulation of other temporal areas in conscious humans has suddenly evoked a change in their "interpretation" of what they are seeing, hearing, or thinking. It is possible that the latter response is a more complex one involving the utilization of several stored "experiences" to apply meaning, recognition or interpretation to immediate events.

OTHER LOCALIZED BRAIN FUNCTIONS

The cerebral cortical area near the junction of the parietal and temporal regions has been shown to function as a critical association area in human brains. Destruction of this area grossly diminishes speech ability and the interpretation of auditory and visual signals. Similarly, the loss of a relatively small area of the frontal (usually left) hemisphere may result in a considerable loss of speech ability.

Many localized responses involving the "primitive cortex" and hypothalamus have been described. The primitive cortex is the area which was associated with olfactory input in ancestral vertebrates. In modern mammals it has been displaced to the medial and ventral brain surfaces by the massive expansion of the "new cerebral cortex." This region has numerous anatomical and physiological associations with the forebrain and new cortex, as well as with the hypothalamus. The expression of such primitive emotions as fear, rage, hunger and sexual display are activated largely through autonomic outflow from the primitive cortex. For example, lesions in the pyriform cortex may result in hypersexual behavior, while destruction of the nearby amygdaloid nuclei often produces a placid behavior (see reference by Gardner for locations). Stimulation or ablation of certain hypothalamic nuclei has produced hyperphagia (overeating) while treatment of other nearby nuclei has produced such a total disinterest in food that starvation ensues.

Other interesting examples of localized brain function include the so-called "pleasure" and "punishment" centers (see reference by Olds). Stimulating electrodes can be permanently placed in certain localized centers of the brain of experimental animals such as rats or monkeys. The stimulating apparatus associated with these electrodes can be arranged in various ways to provide switching circuits in the experimental cage. After an animal discovers the switch he may stimulate himself repeatedly, as if he were receiving a pleasant experience. Sometimes an animal will stimulate himself as many as several thousand times per hour. Localization of the electrodes in other brain areas can elicit an avoidance response, i.e., the animal may carefully avoid the stimulus by pressing an inactivating switch. Many permutations of these self-stimulating experiments are being performed in the study of learning, reinforcement and motivation. The brain areas involved in these studies are several, including the posterior hypothalamus, upper midbrain tegmentum and, anteriorly, the septal and medial forebrain bundle regions (see reference by Gardner).

SPONTANEOUS ACTIVITY OF NERVE CELLS

Low level electrical activity, presumably summated from many active neurons, may be recorded continuously from electrodes placed on the scalp. Such a recording, known as an electroencephalogram (EEG), varies characteristically with location of the electrodes, with the amount of sensory stimulation, and with levels of consciousness. Records from the occipital region of the cerebral cortex show rhythmical "alpha waves" (8-15 cycles/sec.) when the eyes are closed. The provision of visual cues, however, desynchronizes the rhythm, lowers the amplitude and increases the frequency. The correspondence between the level of arousal and the nature of the EEG pattern is well established. As the individual is at first fully alert, then drowsy, lightly asleep and finally in deep sleep, the pattern passes successively from fast, low-amplitude and de-synchronized waves toward slower rhythmical waves of higher amplitude. Although the patterns change perceptibly, activity does not disappear when sensory stimuli are reduced. This indicates that a significant fraction of the activity is spontaneous.

A full understanding of the significance of spontaneous activity in nerve cells is not yet known, but it is clearly a widespread phenomenon in both peripheral and central nervous elements. Several types of autogenic activity are recognized. They range from occasional bursts to extremely rhythmical and continuous firings (remember the electric fish?). Spontaneity is probably a basic property of some few cells, with the activity spreading to neighboring areas. The ultimate effects of such activity depend upon the nature of the interconnections of the units as well as the patterns and frequencies of the discharges.

Spontaneously active cells probably serve several purposes. They may provide a means of continuous facilitation or inhibition of certain synapses having either low or high thresholds. Ongoing activity may be speeded or slowed by other neurons thus providing a complex pattern of impulses of infinite gradation. Autogenic cells are probably intimately involved in most rhythmic motor activities such as breathing, blinking or walking. Finally, they may well be involved in information storage in some reverberating or highly facilitated neuronal circuits of memory.

REFERENCES

BULLOCK, T. H., and HORRIDGE, G. A., *Structure and Function in the Nervous Systems of Invertebrates,* San Francisco: W. H. Freeman and Co., 1965. Vol. I and II.

ECCLES, J. C., *The Physiology of Nerve Cells,* Baltimore: Johns Hopkins Press, 1957.

ECCLES, J. C., "The Synapse." *Scientific American,* January, 1965, p. 56.

GARDNER, E., *Fundamentals of Neurology,* 4th ed. Philadelphia: W. B. Saunders Co., 1963.

GRAY, G. W., "The Great Ravelled Knot." *Scientific American,* October, 1948, p. 26.

KATZ, B., *Nerve, Muscle and Synapse,* New York: McGraw-Hill Co., 1966.

MCLENNAN, H., *Synaptic Transmission,* Philadelphia: W. B. Saunders Co., 1963.

OLDS, J., "Pleasure Centers in the Brain." *Scientific American,* October, 1956, p. 105.

ROEDER, KENNETH D., *Nerve Cells and Insect Behavior,* Cambridge, Massachusetts: Harvard University Press, 1963.

SPERRY, R. W., "The Great Cerebral Commissure." *Scientific American,* January, 1964, p. 42.
SNIDER, R. S., "The Cerebellum." *Scientific American,* August, 1958, p. 84.
WOOLRIDGE, D. E., *The Machinery of the Brain,* New York: McGraw-Hill Book Co., 1963.

CHAPTER 10

Endocrine regulation

INTRODUCTION

In addition to the rapid integration of motor, sensory and memory events by the nervous system, there is also an integration of the slower but profound functions of reproduction, development and growth. Control is exercised over the latter functions largely by the interactions of the various hormones. Our intent in this chapter is to highlight some of the important aspects of hormone action, particularly those that are common to both vertebrate and invertebrate animals.

The endocrine organs release into the blood stream small quantities of substances, the hormones, which influence the metabolic processes of distant target tissues. Pioneers in the study of endocrinology followed a systematic pattern in examining these organs and their hormones. An organ suspected of having an endocrine function was surgically removed and any alterations in the physiology of the animal were noted. In the case of most endocrine glands, characteristic deficiency symptoms soon appeared. For example, if the thyroid were removed, or if it failed to produce its hormone thyroxin, it was observed that growth halted, the metabolic rate diminished, and if very young animals were used, a characteristic body form of small stature, called cretinism, resulted. In another case, the removal of pancreatic islet tissue resulted in the appearance of the symptoms of diabetes mellitus, including the presence of sugar in the urine and other metabolic disorders, which progressively became so debilitating that the subject usually entered into a coma and died. After observing the results of removal of a suspected organ, the next step was either to replace the organ itself by surgical transplant or to administer an extract from the organ. If the deficiency symptoms disappeared, the hormone was generally further characterized by chemical isolation and purification.

In some instances it has been possible to synthesize certain of the hormones in the laboratory. Also, the biosynthesis and metabolic fate of many hormones have now been successfully analyzed. A list of the major mammalian hormones is presented in Table 10-1 at the end of this chapter. Examination of the table will show that the active compounds may be classified chemically as proteins, peptides, amino acid derivatives or steroids.

The more recent studies in endocrinology have concentrated on the mechanisms of hormone action. Although much information has accumulated, we do not yet know in detail how they work or how the circulating levels of the active compounds are regulated. An indication of the dynamic nature of hormone action is illustrated by the number of major physiological processes they affect. These include the regulation of reproduction, growth, development, circulation, metabolism and digestion (Table 10-1).

SOME POSSIBLE MECHANISMS OF HORMONE ACTION

It is now recognized that hormone action is intimately associated with the genetics and embryology of the cell populations which make up organisms. This is to be expected when we consider, as mentioned above, that the hormones function primarily in the regulation of reproduction, development and growth. Each cell of an organism receives the same set of chromosomes and the same complement of genes. The primary mechanism of gene action is the direction of protein synthesis. The various genes, however, are active only in certain cells at specific times. Thus the gene responsible for the synthesis of hemoglobin is operative in red cells but inoperative in kidney cells. Similarly, the gene responsible for the synthesis of the contractile protein myosin is highly active in muscle, but essentially inactive in nerve cells. Variations in both the number and the kind of active genes change the proteins of the various cells both quantitatively and qualitatively, thus providing for growth and tissue differentiation.

The sequence of events leading to protein synthesis begins with the genetic material, the deoxyribonucleic acids (DNA) of the genes. The nucleotide sequence of a DNA molecule is the code for an amino acid sequence of a particular protein molecule. When a gene is active, a molecule of ribonucleic acid (RNA) with a similar code as the DNA of the gene is synthesized within the nucleus. This RNA, referred to as "messenger RNA," moves out of the nucleus and becomes associated with small cytoplasmic bodies, the ribosomes. The ribosomes, so-called because they are composed of ribosomal RNA, hold the messenger RNA while protein synthesis is occurring. There is involved in this process another class of RNA called "transfer RNA." There are specific transfer RNA molecules for each of the 20 amino acids. Transfer RNA molecules are capable of "recognizing" the appropriate amino acid as well as the appropriate code site of the messenger RNA. By means of specific activating enzymes, the appropriate amino acid is attached to the transfer RNA which transports it to the correct site of the messenger RNA. Attachment of the amino acids to each other (peptide bond formation) is the final step in protein synthesis. This scheme provides profound ways of altering structural proteins and enzymes of cells and tissues. If a certain gene were active or inactive at a particular time, the direction and the extent of development and growth could be changed drastically. If hormones could somehow control either the activation of genes or the normal sequence of code transcription from the DNA, they would essentially govern the course of growth and development. Growth hormone, for example, could best operate at this level. Thyroxin is involved in protein synthesis in all higher animals, and in some of the amphibians, it is the "trigger" for the marked growth and differentiation processes associated with metamorphosis. ACTH from the pituitary stimulates adrenal protein synthesis. Estrogens promote rapid protein synthesis in uterine tissue, while testosterone acts similarly in promoting development of male structures and general somatic tissues. The immediate effect of estrogen administration to ovarectomized animals is an elevated production of messenger RNA. This is accompanied by a significant increase in the ribosomal and transfer RNAs. The enhanced protein synthesis is therefore achieved by the increased synthetic machinery which is placed into operation.

Other hormones, for example, insulin from the pancreas, or antidiuretic hormone from the pituitary, appear to act independently of the protein synthetic mechanism. Here, the mode of action seems to lie in altering membrane permeability or in affecting the active transport process, since insulin influences the movement of glucose across cell membranes, while antidiuretic hormone modifies the movement of inorganic ions and water.

REGULATION OF HORMONE LEVELS

Since hormones operate in extremely small concentrations, and since they are capable of modifying the entire biochemistry of tissues, it is not surprising that the circulating levels of these compounds are rigidly controlled. We do not yet know how the organism accomplishes this. In some instances there appears to be a feedback mechanism which controls the level of hormone, such that the endocrine gland's own synthetic mechanism is influenced by the hormone it elaborates. In other cases, something analogous to a receptor-hormone reflex must be operable. For example, coitus results in ovulation in some animals by stimulating the release of lutenizing hormone from the adenohypophysis. In still another reflex-like system, osmotic pressure of the blood flowing through the hypothalamus appears to determine the release of antidiuretic hormone from the pituitary (see Chapter 4).

The reproductive periods of many animals coincide with the seasonal cycles of food abundance, rainfall and favorable temperatures. This means that the level of those hormones that prepare the animal for reproduction and care of the young must also vary seasonally. A major environmental factor governing the reproductive cycle, at least in some animals, appears to be the photoperiod. During the spring, for example, day length increases and night length decreases. Both the level and duration of daylight are thought to be sensed through the eye and perhaps directly by the brain. At any rate, the central nervous system then appears to stimulate the endocrine organs responsible for the synthesis and release of those hormones required for the impending reproductive period.

Some hormones are released or synthesized in a definite order that permits control of a sequential function. After ovulation and fertilization, progesterone is synthesized by the corpus luteum to prepare the uterus for implantation of the ovum; later, it is produced by the placenta to insure maintenance of pregnancy. In some species, relaxin is synthesized and released from the corpus luteum near the termination of pregnancy. Along with estrogen and progesterone this hormone helps to relax the pelvis and prepare the organism for parturition. Similar sequential events lead to the release of a number of hormones that function in the control of the digestive processes.

THE HORMONES WHICH INFLUENCE OTHER ENDOCRINE ORGANS

It is possible to list more than thirty vertebrate hormones and perhaps one-third as many invertebrate hormones. Nearly a dozen of the vertebrate hormones are released from the pituitary gland. Since approximately half of the pituitary hormones influence the growth and secretion of other endocrine organs, this structure has been called the master gland of the endocrine system. Examples of pituitary tropic hormones include thyrotropic hormone (TH), adrenocorticotropic hormone (ACTH), interstitial cell stimulating hormone (ICSH = lutenizing hormone), somatotropic hormone (SH), and follicle-stimulating hormone (FSH). Another endocrine gland that elaborates several hormones is the adrenal cortex. Its products include principally cortisone, corticosterone (hydrocortisone, cortisol) and aldosterone. Their synthesis and release are largely influenced by the ACTH of the pituitary.

NEUROSECRETION: THE INTERACTION OF THE NERVOUS SYSTEM AND THE ENDOCRINE ORGANS

A close functional relationship is maintained between the pituitary and the hypothalamus of the brain. In fact, some of the hormones released by the pituitary are synthesized by special neurosecretory cells within the hypothalamus. The process of neurosecretion furnishes an interesting and obvious example of hybrid integration involving both the nervous and endocrine organs. Here, the synthesis of the hormone occurs in the cell bodies of the neurosecretory neurons. The hormone, or its precursor substance, is transported along the axons of the neurons to a distant site where it is released into the circulation. As is the case with the other hormones, the site of action of neurosecretions is generally some distance from the site of release, and they are transported as usual by the circulation. Neurosecretion in the vertebrates is exemplified by the processes occurring in the neurohypophysis. This portion of the pituitary receives several neurosecretory tracts, that is, axon bundles from the hypothalamus. The hormones released from this lobe, namely antidiuretic hormone and oxytocin, are synthesized in the hypothalamus and transported to the site of release along the axons of the neurosecretory tracts. Neurosecretion may be considered a logical extension of the normal synthesis of transmitter which is typical of virtually all nerve cells. In fact, norepinephrine is both a transmitter for some synapses and a hormone elaborated by the adrenal medulla. It should be pointed out that in the arthropods, the majority of the endocrine structures are neurosecretory in nature and are situated in the major centers of the nervous system. In a few cases, invertebrate neurosecretory neurons have been shown to be capable of producing action potentials. This lends further evidence to the notion that the endocrine function of nerve cells is not far removed from that characteristic of typical nervous tissue.

INVERTEBRATE ENDOCRINOLOGY

The vertebrate hormones, with the exception of some of the neuro-transmitters, do not function in invertebrate animals. Instead, the invertebrates produce their own set of hormones from their own characteristic endocrine glands. This indicates that there is nothing universal about the action of hormone molecules alone; it is the ability of the tissues to react as well as the chemical nature of the hormone that is important.

There are a number of similarities between vertebrate and invertebrate hormone systems in their overall organization and mode of action. For example, in both groups, hierarchies are established with some hormones having a tropic function for others. Equally common are the synergistic and antagonistic hormones which seem to increase the sensitivity of control. Perhaps the most striking similarity is the close cooperation that is seen between the various nervous and endocrine centers.

One of the best known invertebrate endocrine systems is that regulating growth and development in insects. As an example, we will consider the development of the large silkworm moth *Halaphora cercropia* since it has been used for much of the detailed work on insect development. Pioneer work on the large blood-sucking bug, *Rhodnius*, however, laid the ground work for the studies we are about to describe.

Silkworm moths undergo several molts as larvae (caterpillars), each stage being characterized by marked growth but little change in appearance. The last larval molt is accompanied by a metamorphosis into the pupa, the stage during which the adult tissues are organized. At the final molt a second and even more drastic metamorphosis occurs which gives rise to the adult. This sequence of events is controlled by the inter--action of three primary endocrine glands, the brain-corpora cardiaca, the corpora allata and the prothoracic glands (Fig. 10-1). A series of simple but elegant experiments has shown how these centers interact. If a fine thread is tied around the neck of an early larva to prevent any hormone produced by the brain from reaching the body tissues, the animal will fail to grow and to pupate. If a similar ligature is placed on an older larva, it will continue to grow and form a pupa. These experiments indicate that a hormone from the head region is released at a critical time to carry the development process forward. We now know that this substance, called *brain hormone* (BH), is synthesized by neurosecretory cells located in the brain. Axons from the cells transport brain hormone to the corpora cardiaca for storage and release. The next step is to ligature the silkworm just posterior to the prothoracic glands. The anterior end of the animal will show normal development to pupation while the tail end will fail to grow and will remain larval. Such treatment confines

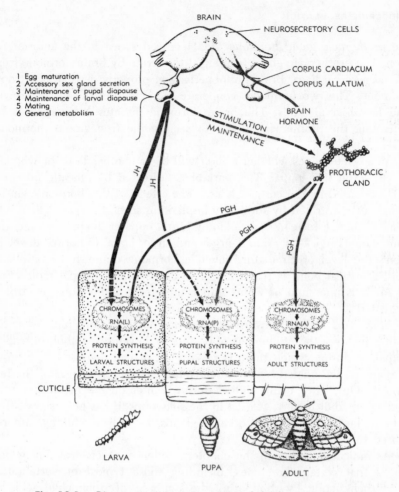

Fig. 10-1. Diagrammatic representation of the hormonal control of growth and metamorphosis in the silkworm moth. Three hormones interact in this scheme, brain hormone, prothoracic gland hormone (PGH) and juvenile hormone (JH). Brain hormone initiates the process by activating the prothoracic glands. Juvenile hormone determines the form the molts will take; in its presence there are larval-larval molts. When it diminishes the animal molts from larva to pupa. As described in the text, these hormones are presumed to act on the protein synthetic mechanisms directly. Juvenile hormone along with prothoracic gland hormone provides RNA molecules which give rise to larval (L) proteins. In the absence of juvenile hormone, pupal (P) and adult (A) proteins predominate. The several functions ascribed to the corpora allata are shown at the upper left. (From L. I. Gilbert, "Hormones Controlling Reproduction and Molting in Invertebrates," in: **Comparative Endocrinology,** Vol. II, U. S. Von Euler and H. Heller, editors, New York, Academic Press, Inc., 1963.)

the *prothoracic gland hormone* (PGH or ecdysone) to the anterior region. The prothoracic gland is induced to secrete by brain hormone from the corpora cardiaca. Brain hormone is then properly classed as a tropic hormone. The two hormones cooperate in regulating the larval growth and larval-larval molts. The brain hormone initiates the responses by activating the prothoracic glands to secrete the true growth hormone, PGH.

What determines whether a molt will be to another larva or whether it will result in a pupa? This variable is directed by *juvenile hormone* (JH) released by the corpora allata. The effects of this hormone can be clearly demonstrated by surgically implanting several corpora allata into a larval animal. Instead of developing into a pupa at the proper time, the animal molts repeatedly into a larger and larger larva. In normal development, the level of circulating juvenile hormone diminishes continually until a critical point is reached which allows a larval-pupal molt (Fig. 10-1). It is uncertain how this important aspect of hormonal control is regulated.

Silkworms generally overwinter in the pupal stage. Preparation for winter involves the attainment of a state of lowered metabolism, called diapause, during which there is no growth or cell divisions. The onset of diapause is signaled by the diminishing day length typical of the fall months. Only after being chilled during winter do the pupae begin to synthesize adult tissues. At least in the silkworms, it has been shown that a brain factor and the prothoracic glands, as well as chilling, are required to break diapause.

As indicated earlier in the chapter, evidence is accumulating which shows that certain hormones, including those typical of vertebrates, exert their action by stimulating the synthesis of ribonucleic acids in the nuclei of target cells. This leads, as we have seen, to the synthesis of specific proteins and to growth. If the newly synthesized proteins appear in quantity and if they are different from those previously present, the organism might not only grow, but show a change ... morphology. This is assumed to be the major means of action of both PGH and juvenile hormone. According to this scheme, prothoracic gland hormone in cooperation with juvenile hormone stimulates the nuclear synthesis of those messenger RNA molecules which give rise to larval proteins. As a result, larval tissues are induced to grow and larval molts follow. In the absence of juvenile hormone, PGH stimulates the production of RNAs which provide adult proteins. The adult proteins are so different from those typical of the larva, that their presence leads to the spectacular metamorphosis seen at emergence.

TABLE 10-1

Major Mammalian Hormones

Gland	Hormones	Chemical Nature and Major Effects
Pituitary Adenohypophysis	growth hormone (GH)	protein—promotes general protein synthesis and growth
	thyrotropin (TH)	protein—promotes synthesis and release of thyroid hormone
	adrenocorticotropin (ACTH)	protein—affects synthesis or release of adrenal cortical steroids
	lutenizing hormone (LH) or inter- stitial cell stimulating hormone (ISCH)	protein—promotes growth of ovarian follicle and progesterone secretion in female, stimulates interstitial tissues of testes and androgen secretion in male
	follicle stimulating hormone (FSH)	protein—enhances follicle develop- ment, secretion of estrogen and ovulation in female, promotes de- velopment of seminiferous tubules and spermatogenesis in males
	luteotropin = prolactin (LTH)	protein—stimulates progesterone secretion by corpus luteum, mam- mary growth and milk secretion
Neurohypophysis	antidiuretic hormone (ADH) = vasopressin	peptide—promotes water reabsorp- tion in kidney, alters blood pres- sure
	oxytocin	peptide—promotes contraction of smooth muscles, particularly of the uterus, stimulates milk ejection
Adrenal Cortex	corticosterone	steroid—promotes glucose synthesis from protein, protein metabolism, lymphocytosis, and resistance to infection and stress
	cortisone and hydrocortisone	steroids—have some effects similar to those of corticosterone, but also modify sodium and water transport in several tissues
	aldosterone	steroid—stimulates active trans- port of Na^+ across membranes
Adrenal Medulla	epinephrine = adrenalin	amino acid derivative—promotes contraction of smooth and cardiac muscle, increases heart rate, stimulates conversion of glycogen to glucose

Gland	Hormones	Chemical Nature and Major Effects
Adrenal Medulla (con't)	norephinephrine	amino acid derivative—has effects similar to those of epinephrine but more effective in contracting the arterioles to raise blood pressure
Pancreas Islets of Langerhans	insulin (anti-diabetes hormone)	protein—controls carbohydrate regulation and utilization
	glucagon	peptide—increases utilization of glucose from glycogen stores
Thyroid	thyroxine	amino acid derivative—enhances general metabolic rate of tissues stimulates protein synthesis in all animals and metamorphosis in amphibians
Parathyroid	parathormone	protein—regulates calcium and phosphate metabolism of bone and other tissue
Testis	testosterone (from interstitial cells)	steroid—influences maturation and function of testes and development of secondary sexual characteristics
Ovary	estrone + estradiol (estrogens)	steroids—influences maturation and function of ovaries and development of secondary sexual characteristics
Corpus Luteum	progesterone	steroid—prepares uterus for implantation of ovum and maintenance of pregnancy
	relaxin	protein—alters muscle tone, relaxes pubic symphysis preceding parturition in some mammals
Placenta	estrogens progesterone lutenizing hormone follicle stimulating hormone (FSH)	see above table
Stomach	gastrin	peptide—enhances the secretion of hydrochloric acid by parietal cells of stomach
Duodenum	secretin	promotes secretion of bicarbonate by the pancreas
	pancreozymin	stimulates secretion of digestive enzymes by pancreas
	enterogastrone	inhibits stomach mobility and secretion
	cholecystokinin	promotes emptying of gall bladder by contraction

Some exciting evidence for the activation of genes by these insect hormones has been obtained recently by direct cytological observation. The salivary glands of some larval insects have giant chromosomes that can be observed readily and mapped under the microscope. During active synthesis of RNA, large visible puffs (of RNA) appear on these chromosomes, presumably at the sites where the genes are most active. During normal development, chromosome puffs appear that are characteristic of certain stages of growth of the insect. Prothoracic gland hormone has now been demonstrated to induce chromosome puffing that is typical of that which characterizes the larval-pupal molt.

It is thus possible to conceive of a scheme whereby specific hormones on reaching their target cells activate specific genes within those cells. The resulting messenger RNA controls the production of specific proteins that are responsible for the growth and differentiation of the organ in question, or, in some cases, perhaps even of the entire organism. Different hormones control the activities of different organs. Some hormones may act only at certain critical times in the development of the organism; others may exert their influences throughout most of the life span. Although details may differ, this generalized scheme is probably operative in both vertebrates and invertebrates.

REFERENCES

CARLISLE, D. B., and KNOWLES, F., *Endocrine Control in Crustaceans*, Cambridge, England: Cambridge University Press, 1959.

DAVIDSON, E. H., "Hormones and Genes." *Scientific American*, June, 1965, p. 36.

GORBMAN, A., and BERN, H. A., *A Textbook of Comparative Endrocrinology*, New York: John Wiley and Sons, Inc., 1962.

RUCH, T. C., and FULTON, J. F., (eds.), *Medical Physiology and Biophysics*, 18th ed. Philadelphia: W. B. Saunders Co., 1960. Ch. 51-58, pp. 1040-1178.

ROCKSTEIN, M., (ed.), *The Physiology of Insecta*, New York: Academic Press, 1965. Vol. I, Ch. 5, pp. 149-225.

SCHEER, B. T., *Animal Physiology*, New York: John Wiley and Sons, Inc., 1963. Ch. 13, pp. 281-309.

WHITE, A., HANDLER, P., and SMITH, E. L., *Principles of Biochemistry*. 3rd ed. New York: McGraw-Hill Book Co., 1964. Ch. 45-51.

Conclusion

In the span of about a century since the study of physiology has existed as a separate discipline, we have accumulated a large body of knowledge about the form and function of animals. However, it is safe to say that our understanding of animal physiology is still far from complete. In fact, some of the most basic principles and the most universal phenomena have proven to be the most elusive. A fitting conclusion to a short book of this type might be to point out a few of the many unsolved problems in biology.

Let us begin at the cellular level with the problem of gene action. What turns genes on and off? How does gene expression manage to direct cell growth, cell division and specialization? How do these developing cells affect one another as they organize into tissues and organs? How do hormones initiate and control these processes? Once a cell has been formed we are still perplexed by many of the functions of its parts, even those that appear deceptively simple. We know how important both external and internal membranes are to the normal functioning of cells. We know, too, that membranes differ in various types of cells within an organism and that there may be specialized areas on the surface of a single cell. How do membranes form, what causes them to differentiate, and how are they repaired and maintained? What could be a more significant problem for all of biology than the details of oxidative phosphorylation? This process, which occurs in the membranes of mitochondria, is an almost ubiquitous mechanism for providing the energy of life in the form of phosphorylated compounds such as ATP. Similarly, we do not know how the membrane achieves active transport, and this too is a universal phenomenon of living organisms. The membranes of nerve and muscle present special problems. How does a nerve membrane secrete transmitter in response to an incoming action potential along its axon? How are the contractile events of muscles coupled to the electrical changes of their membranes?

As we move to a higher level of organization more questions arise, partly as a result of the association of cells into tissues and organs. How does a network of variously coupled neurons working together provide a computer and read-out system of unmatched versatility? Only at a very superficial level do we know how some of the components of the brain computer work — or with what other components they are functionally associated. Every complex animal has such a neuronal mass; should we attack this problem by studying the simplest ones? Some workers think so, while others believe the mechanisms underlying the functions of the brains of higher animals are unique and require direct observation. In a related problem, what do we know about the genetics and evolution of behavior? Perhaps a great deal, but not enough to predict the course of events. Would it be valuable to man's knowledge to be able to make these predictions?

What underlies a process such as temperature compensation, which occurs to a varying extent in virtually every animal? What is the molecular basis of the universal sense of time — the biological clock? Is the clock located in some specific organ or structure? Unicellular animals show circadian rhythms; does this mean that all cells of more complex organisms have such a clock? If they do, how are they synchronized to time the activities of whole animals? This brings us to another perplexing problem, one of almost philosophic import, and that is, why do organisms age? For that matter, is it mandatory that they do so?

The queries above represent a few of the topics that are under consideration in modern biology. Some of them appear invincible now, yet problems of similar complexity were solved quickly in the past by the appropriate experimental approach. We can confidently expect their solution in the future, but with this advance will come new problems. It would be dull indeed if there were no more questions to ask.

Index

(Page numbers in boldface refer to illustrations.)

149

gain and loss factors, 74, 75
units of, 33
heamtocrit, 15
hemocyanin, 59, 60, 62
hemoglobin, 59-61
Henle's loop, 37, **38**, 44
hibernation, 79-81
homeotherm, 71, 73
hormones, chemical nature, 136, 140,
143, 144
controlling digestion, 138, 144
controlling muscle, 95
influencing protein synthesis, 136, 137
140, 141, 142, 145
levels in circulation, 138
list and functions, 143, 144
tropic, 139, **140**
hydrolysis, 13, 30
5-hydroxytryptamine, 121
hypothalamus, 74, 77, 80, 112, 129, 132,
139

imprinting, 111
indirect calorimetry, 67
infrared, detection by snakes, 6, 78
inhibition, **120**, 121, 123, 125, 128
in retina, 105
of muscle, 92, 93
insect development, hormone control,
140, **141**, 142
insect muscle, **92**, 93, 94
insulation, 74, 77
interneuron, **125**
intestine, absorption from, 32, 34, **35**
enzymes, **35**
microorganisms of, 29, 31, 36
interstitial fluid, 14-16
intracellular fluid, 14-16
invertebrate hormones, 140
ionic distribution, nerve, **101**, 102

juvenile hormone, 140, **141**, 142

kangaroo rat, 43, 44
kidney, 37-45
concentrating mechanisms in, 41, 43,
44, **45**

length of blood vessels, resistance effects,
17, 18
light, action on rhodopsin, 104, 105, **106**,
107
lipids (fats), caloric value, 67, 69
digestion, 30
membranes, 7, 10, **11**
permeability, 10, **11**, 30
requirements in diet, 33
lung, 54, **55**
area of surfaces, 54
dead space, 55
stretch receptors, 54
ventilation, 55, 56

lymph, 24, 25
lymphatic vessels, **24**, 25, 26

marine birds, osmoregulation, 46, **47**
mechanoreceptors, 99, 112 (see proprioceptors)
medulla, 54, 112
membrane, structure and permeability,
7, **11**
membrane potential, electroplaques, 96,
97
nerve, 102, **103**, 120
messenger RNA, 137, 142, 145
metabolites, exchange in capillaries, **24**,
25
metamorphosis, amphibian, 137
insect, 140, **141**, 142
mineral, requirements, 32, 33
mitochrondria, 83, 85
motor control, 124, **124**, 127, 128, **129**,
133
motor cortex, 123, **124**, 128, **129**
motor neuron, 83, 88, 89, **90**, 91, **92**, 124
impulse frequency in, 90, 91, 93
motor unit, muscle, **90**, 91, **124**
muscle, 82-98
contractile proteins, 5, 87
dependency upon nerve, 95
muscle fibers (striated) 83, **84**
myofibrils, 83, **84**, 85, 86, 87
myogenic heart, 19
myoneural junction, 83, 92, 120
myosin, **86**, 87, 136
bridges, **86**, 87, 88

nasal glands, 5, 46, **47**
navigation, 3, 111
nephron, 37, **38**, 45
nerve impulse, 100, 101, 102, **103**, 121
frequency, **122**, 123
velocity of conduction, 6, 104
nervous system, 118-133
neurogenic heart, 19
neurosecretion, 139, 140
neurotransmitter, 89, 92, 119-121
nitrogen, 52, 53, 58
norepinephrine, 95, 121, 144
nutrition, 28-36

omnivore, digestive processes, 34, **35**
osmoreceptors, 44, 46, 112, 138
osmoregulation, 46, **47**, **48**, 49
osmotic pressure, **23**, 24
osmotic reabsorption, capillaries, **24**
kidney, 40, 44, **45**
oxygen
biological oxidations, 4, **12**, 50, 51, 66
carried by hemocyanin, 62
carried by hemoglobin, 60
consumption rates of animals, 70
environmental, 52, 53
oxygen capacity, 59, 60, 61
oxygen consumption, body size, 70, 71